WHAT BEING CATHOLIC MEANS TO ME

Edited by John Littleton and Eamon Maher

What Being Catholic Means to Me

the columba press

First published in 2009 by
the columba press
55A Spruce Avenue, Stillorgan Industrial Park,
Blackrock, Co Dublin

Cover by Bill Bolger
Origination by The Columba Press
Printed in Ireland by ColourBooks Ltd, Dublin

ISBN 978-1-85607-6735-3

Table of Contents

Introduction

Many of the contributors to this book remarked how difficult it was to write about something as personal as their Catholic heritage, which most – excepting those who have dedicated their life to Roman Catholicism as priests or religious – had never really thought about in any serious way. As editors, we left things as open as we could, merely telling those who agreed with our approach to situate themselves in relation to age and family background in order for readers to be able to grasp the period during which they grew up and how a belief system took root in them or not, as the case may be. Clearly people who were born well before the seismic event that was Vatican II (1962-1965) would have had a very different experience of Catholicism from those born after it. Similarly, those from a rural background may have been exposed to a religion that was rooted in the soil, where the main religious feasts mirrored those of the land and of the seasons, where Sunday was in a real sense a day of rest, the Mass one of the few occasions where one met up with members of the wider community. Equally, they may have been more likely to engage in the most common family prayer at that time, the Rosary, than their counterparts in the cities. That said, a huge number of Irish citizens who ended up in the main cities were originally from the countryside and brought their belief system and religious practices with them.

With a topic as emotive as one's religious beliefs, it is important, therefore, not to generalise, demean, idolise or trivialise. Those who feature in this book displayed admirable courage and honesty in tackling the subject and we as editors are very grateful to them for taking the time and the risk to share their thoughts with a wider public.

Our aim was to get as broad a cross-section of opinion as possible. In that, we feel that we have succeeded to a reasonable extent. It is true that the largest single group consists of priests, but those included display a refreshingly disparate approach to the question of what being Catholic means to them. Also, because they are 'religious professionals', priests have an added interest in the issues that are broached in this book. Likewise, journalists feature strongly, but they are generally people who are used to putting forward their opinions in written and oral form and so it was not all that surprising that they should accede to our request. We were acutely conscious of gender balance and, with this in mind, we asked many women to contribute. It has often been stated how Irish women have displayed a fierce loyalty and commitment to Catholicism, which was in no small way responsible for the flowering of that religious tradition in this country. Sadly, we do not have an equal number of male and female contributors, but the women write with great passion and honesty and raise some serious questions about how they sometimes feel disenfranchised within the Church structures, or alienated by the patriarchal hierarchy. There can be no doubt that women will have to play a significant role if there is to be any regeneration of the Church as an organisation capable of playing a meaningful role in post-Celtic Tiger Ireland.

Given the traditionally strong links between Church and State in Ireland, it is an advantage to have the views of some young and 'less young' politicians. As our legislators, politicians are responsible for setting up Commissions of Inquiry into alleged abuses and for investigating instances where the rights of individuals and groups have been infringed.

Poetry has often been described as the place where a religious sensibility can find a hospitable environment and hence it is important that we have a poet and creative writer included. As one of our contributors, Mark Patrick Hederman, observes elsewhere: 'Through the language of poetry, the work of art, a breath beyond the breathing space of the artist can impress itself upon our hearing.'[1] According to Hederman, metaphysical poetry is the only real contact with Being, the only ontological language available in contemporary culture, and Mary O'Donnell's reflections capture this sensitivity extremely well.

Psychiatry is another area of vital importance to our understanding of Irish Catholicism, and perhaps to some of its less savoury aspects, and so the inclusion of an expert in this area is also necessary and significant.

One regret we have is the absence of a voice from within the hierarchy. Several bishops were approached, one gave positive indications that he might contribute, but in the end none came forward. With our previous two books, we have had a similar experience. One of our intentions is to stimulate a dialogue about Irish Catholicism. It is difficult to do this without some of the main stakeholders getting involved and expressing their views.

This book appears shortly after the publication of the Commission of Inquiry into Child Abuse Report (popularly referred to as the Ryan Report) and when the findings of the investigation into the handling of clerical sex abuse in the Dublin Archdiocese are about to be made public. These are difficult times for anyone to be a Catholic in Ireland. There is a natural tendency to paint everyone with the same brush. But being Catholic means something different for each and every one of us. Each person interprets the Gospel in his or her particular way. Each experiences the rituals of the Church, the ministry of priests and lay people, the transmission of the word, as individuals who are part of a wider community. The fact that the Church is undergoing serious upheaval in Ireland is not in itself a valid reason for everyone to get up and leave it. Equally, no one should stay a member simply because of habit or the absence of a viable alternative. For far too long, Irish people were Catholics almost by accident. As Fintan O'Toole remarked:

> Catholicism in Ireland has been a matter of public identity more than of private faith. For most of its history, the

---

1. Mark Patrick Hederman, *The Haunted Inkwell* (Dublin: The Columba Press, 2001), p 34.

> Republic of Ireland was essentially a Catholic state, one in which the limits of the law and of behaviour were set by church orthodoxy and the beliefs of the Catholic bishops.[2]

This is patently no longer the case, especially when it comes to the power of the bishops to dictate how individuals should behave in their public or private lives. Much has happened in the last twenty years that has damaged the reputation of the Catholic Church across the globe. There is a lot of soul-searching among Catholics as to how they can continue to claim membership of a Church that refuses to admit women priests, that continues to hold firm on the interdiction of artificial means of contraception, that demonstrates a condemnatory attitude towards homosexual practices, that will not allow its priests to marry, that refuses the sacraments to those whose marriages have broken down and are in second relationships. If one claims to be a Catholic, does that mean that one accepts all these positions? If we are to believe the contributors to this book, being Catholic is considerably more than just conforming to dogmas that are handed down from 'on high'. It is about carefully thinking through the positives and negatives that are contingent on adherence to a religious tradition that can bring both succour and suffering to its members, that can be caring and uncaring, proud and humble, corrupt and uplifting.

The tradition of the Catholic intellectual never took root in Ireland in the way in did in other European countries. Ireland's leading sociologist of religion, Tom Inglis, explained this lacuna in his groundbreaking study, *Moral Monopoly: The Catholic Church in Modern Irish Society*:

> The dominance of 'the simple faith' has meant that many Irish Catholics have not developed an intellectual interest in, or critical attitude towards, their religion. While there have been frequent public debates and critical assessments made of the State, political parties, trade unions and other national organ-

---

2. Fintan O'Toole, *The Ex-Isle of Ireland* (Dublin: New Island Books, 1997), p 15.

isations, the Catholic Church has, until recently, remained aloof from rigorous criticism and public accountability.[3]

Mutatis mutandis – how things have changed! This lack of an intellectual grasp of their faith by Irish people led, in our view, to the massive desertion of Catholic churches in the wake of the various scandals involving Bishop Eamonn Casey and Father Michael Cleary, followed by the clerical abuse revelations, the Ferns and Ryan Reports, etc. People were horrified that so-called 'men of the cloth' could behave in such a disreputable manner and did not possess a strong enough interior life to withstand what they viewed as a betrayal of trust. The Church was also partly to blame in that it preferred not to be challenged on doctrinal matters and thus denied people the freedom of thought that is essential to genuine faith. Writing about rural Brittany during the 1930s and 1940s, the French priest writer Jean Sulivan wrote in his memoir, *Anticipate Every Goodbye*:

> If the Church had taken the concept of freedom seriously, the changes in the world would not have threatened Christianity in any way. The only thing that would have come under pressure was that which was no longer valid, having been linked to a past when power and prestige were the dominant features of the institutional Church. Many of those who refuse the truth are really refusing falsified truths, which undermine a person's conscience.[4]

The relevance of Sulivan's pronouncements to the Ireland of today is remarkable, given that these lines were written more than four decades ago. Moving from a position of power and prestige to one of insignificance and humiliation cannot have been easy for the Catholic Church in Ireland. However, what anyone who remains a Catholic – in whatever loose manner that may be – must do, is accept that the institution is subject to the

---

3. Tom Inglis, *Moral Monopoly: The Catholic Church in Modern Irish Society* (Dublin: Gill and Macmillan, 1987), p 2.

4. Jean Sulivan, *Anticipate Every Goodbye*, trs Eamon Maher (Dublin: Veritas, 2000), p 52.

same human failings as any institution. It may profess lofty ideals and aspirations, preach about love, grace and eternity, but ultimately it is run by men who are bedeviled by the same hopes and ambitions as anyone else and who thus inevitably fall short of the example of Jesus of Nazareth. Being Catholic means being aware of all the good and bad that belonging to such a grouping entails. It is a complex, frustrating, uplifting, depressing, para-doxical journey with, for some, an uncertain destination. But really, you will want to read through the pages that follow and appreciate for yourselves what it entails for our contributors.

In conclusion, we wish to thank all the contributors for their wonderful co-operation in this enterprise. It was delightful to work with them. We acknowledge the indefatigable Seán O Boyle and his committed staff at The Columba Press whose pro-fessionalism and energy never cease to amaze us.

John Littleton and Eamon Maher

An Irish Catholic Agnostic

Patsy McGarry

I was a very devout youngster, even if ours was not a particularly religious household. As soon as I could walk my mother used to take me to early Mass on a Sunday morning in Frenchpark, north-west Roscommon, on her bike. She had a special 'baby chair' put where the carrier behind the saddle should be. Other Sundays I'd go to second Mass in Frenchpark with my father in his Morris Minor, me, my brothers and my sister, Mary. Then we'd end up in the choir of the church upstairs where the men would be and where Frankie Martin used to play the organ and sing the hymns in his rich baritone voice. 'God Almighty, he's a great voice,' the men would say as they chatted among themselves during the Mass. And he had. They'd talk away, then stop and get on their knees in reverent silence during the consecration. When it was over they'd resume the conversations again.

After Mass we'd head to Kelly's pub up the street where, as the men had pints, we kids ate Tayto crisps from a grease-proof packet with an opaque window, and drank lemonade. Then we'd go home for the dinner.

My grandfather and godfather, Patsy, who lived with us, rarely went to Mass. He was in his 80s by then. But he used to pray. As a child it took me some time to understand who those private conversations were with, when he thought no one was around. Once, much later, he caught me in somewhat similar silent mode but misunderstood. He said to me: 'Patsy, don't think so much.' There was wisdom there.

He was, like my father, sceptical of clergy. The reasons were political. My father, for instance, though always respectful of priests, and in a way which sometimes amazed me – because he seemed to have so little respect for anyone in authority – never got over the fact that his idol (there is no other word!) Éamon de Valera had been excommunicated twice by the Catholic Church. In all my life, I would have to say that Dev was the only person on this planet my father never had a bad word for. He was very fair where everyone else was concerned, though.

But my grandfather's reserve about clergy in politics was compounded by an experience he had at a Station Mass in a neighbour's house, sometime in the 1930s. It was in Toolan's, just up the hill behind us in Mullen. My grandfather had been a founder member of the local Fianna Fáil Cumann, the previous decade. The usual kerfuffle took place in Toolan's that morning as last minute preparations for the Stations were underway, right up to when the priest arrived. As with most Fianna Fáilers at the time, my grandfather was convinced that nearly all clergy supported Fine Gael. There was an election in the air. So, I suspect, he might have been prepared for what was to happen.

At the Station in Toolan's, when it came to the homily that morning, the same priest did not beat about the bush. He excoriated Fianna Fáil and encouraged the attendance to vote for the local Fine Gael candidate. Driven to fury by this, my grandfather did the unthinkable – he stood up and interrupted the sermon. He asked the priest, 'Father, where does it say that in the gospel?' The priest became apoplectic. He ranted and raved and blew steam left, right and centre before, eventually, settling down to continue the Mass. However, at its end, and as everyone rose to leave, my grandfather was stuck to his chair. It had been painted that morning and was still wet when he sat on it. But the story went around that 'Patsy McGarry was stuck to the chair by the priest for interrupting his sermon. Did ya ever hear the like?'

My teacher Mrs Molly Ford (now in her 90s) was and remains a devout Catholic. She had a profound influence on me. The Jesuits used say: 'Give us the boy until he is seven and we'll have the man for life', or sentiments to that effect. Mrs Ford taught me until I was ten. That was at a small one-teacher country school in Mullen, which was walking distance from our house. One of my earliest memories involves Mrs Ford. She used to stop at the back of our house at a stile there to talk to my mother on her way home from school. One day they were discussing the antics of one of the pupils who that day had actually stood up on a desk in the classroom. Mrs Ford turned to me and said: 'Patsy, when you come to school, sure you'll never do anything like that?' And I said: 'No, Mrs Ford.' And I meant it. I already liked the woman. I was also well warned by my mother. I would be a good little boy. And I was.

I was also the eldest in our family, a role I took seriously, and enjoyed particularly when it came to enforcing the law on my younger siblings. At school I took my lessons seriously too, and my catechism. The latter was central to my arriving at a situation where, in Mrs Ford's eye, I could do no wrong. The diocesan examiner arrived at the school one day to check on our knowledge of Christian doctrine. The priest asked us what was the name of the husband of Elizabeth, cousin of the Virgin Mary and mother of St John. The class was dumb as Zachary. I raised my hand and said 'Zachary, Father.' Mrs Ford was beside herself with delight and the priest was very pleased indeed. He gave me one of those small cards they used to hand out on occasions like that. It had an image of the crucified Christ looking down on the globe by (as I would discover years later) Salvador Dali.

But my belief soon evolved from the classroom and became a full-blown personal relationship with God. It was the most important thing to me, even before family or friends. In those times I prayed as easily as I drew breath, sometimes using formal prayers, more frequently just talking directly to God. I remember once lying on dry heather in the bog across the fields from our house where I was minding our cattle that summer afternoon as they ate what sweet grass they could find in those vast empty acres. I was about eight or nine and content as could be. There was nothing but blue sky above with great white clouds which revealed continents and oceans and armadas to me. There was a lark somewhere in that infinity too, warbling notes as fully rounded as marbles. And in the background, the steady munch, munch, munch of the cattle as they tugged at and ate the grass. It was some years later before I broke down the ingredients of such contentment. They were simple: God, something amorphous to tease my mind, and a steady rhythm in the background. In that moment and many similar others as a child, I realised how happy I was. I had discovered the joy of solitude.

I became a generous kid with a prickly conscience which punctured my spirit if I did not do what I believed was right, and with a full heart. It meant that one November afternoon, for instance, I rescued from purgatory all my deceased relatives and neighbours during a series of visits to the parish church in Frenchpark, where I secured a plenary indulgence for each. Anyone seeing that small boy entering and leaving the church at regular intervals – to end and begin each visit separately, so as to secure each plenary indulgence – must have been intrigued as to what was going on. Had they known they would probably have been even more fascinated.

As I approached the age of ten, I was clear that when I grew up I would be a priest. By then too Mrs Ford was training me to be an altar boy. This began shortly after one huge crisis in our school when, at Mass in Frenchpark one Sunday, Father Donnellan found himself with no altar boys to serve the Mass. On the altar that morning Father Donnellan lost his temper completely, so much so that altar boys in the congregation were too terrified to offer their assistance. They included some of the older boys in Mullen school. The following day Mrs Ford did not conceal her anger at these lads. Some time later that week she began training me to be an altar boy. I was the real 'teacher's pet'. And worse, I was proud of it! But I never did serve Mass. We had left Mullen before my training was complete and, at ten, I was considered too old to train as an altar boy in Ballaghaderreen.

One of the main reasons my father moved us to Ballaghaderreen was its schools. It had a convent with secondary and primary schools, the De La Salle Brothers' primary school for boys, the Vocational School, and St Nathy's College for boys. It is a cathedral town, seat of the Bishop of Achonry. The town seemed full of clergy, with nuns, brothers and priests. Almost all teachers in the convent and in St Nathy's were clergy. Men saluted the priests and brothers when they met them on the street. The culture I encountered in Ballaghaderreen was of a more robust kind than that in Mullen where, though there was corporal punishment in the school, it hardly measured up to what was meted out in the Brothers' and, to a lesser extent, at St Nathy's. Even then I knew it was wrong, particularly the ritual humiliation a few fellow pupils were put through and the sheer mindless savagery of some of it.

The 10 o'clock children's Mass on Sundays in Ballaghaderreen was usually said by Bishop James Fergus who used tell us boys and girls about what was going on at the Second Vatican Council, which he was then attending. I became very interested in the Council and what was happening there. I was particularly enthused by its emphasis on ecumenism. Even at a young age I had found it impossible to accept that a God of love would damn all outside of the Catholic faithful. This was emphasised for me when the son of the only Protestant (Church of Ireland) family in the town sat beside me at the Brothers' school. He used to be excused for prayers and catechism classes. I could not believe that someone so polite and inoffensive was destined for hell or even eternal deprivation of the beatific vision. This belief, in later years, became extended beyond the Christian denominations to people of other faiths and eventually included people of all faiths and of none. It seemed utterly contradictory to me that a God of love could reject anything of his creation. Karl Marx once said: 'Nothing human is alien to me.' I could not see how God would feel otherwise, allowing for the evil that humans do. There is generally a reason.

Of great interest to me was the Vatican Council document *Gaudium et Spes* (the *Pastoral Constitution on the Church in the Modern World*). It was published in 1965. I was attending St Nathy's by then and it was while there I studied that document in some detail. It re-shaped my Catholicism into something much more pro-active. *Gaudium et Spes* educated me in ideas of social justice, to which I was strongly drawn.

Throughout my teens, Catholicism totally dominated my thinking in areas of sexuality, as in so much else, and I was comfortable with that, particularly with its emphasis on the dignity of every person. It was a gentler teaching on sexuality than what had been the norm not too long before. No one told us masturbation would make us blind, for instance, though it was discouraged as an abuse of our own bodies, temples of the Holy Ghost. Our sex education classes, literally, became comic. This was hardly surprising as a celibate instructed the virginal in what was wholly theoretical. We had to submit anonymous notes to the priest concerned with our queries about matters sexual. I will always remember his response to one such query. He read it aloud, as he did all: 'How long does it (intercourse) last?' To which he replied: 'I don't know, boy. I never experienced it.'

The Church's teaching on sexuality led me, very early on, to accept and respect the complete equality of women and, later, of gay men and lesbian women. It would make me feel in later years that it was being inconsistent with the spirit of its own teaching on the unique dignity of every man and woman when it condemned homosexuality, as it still does.

Even as my teens progressed, and I fell in and out of love, the idea of priesthood was never far from my mind. My faith had deepened as my understanding of it had become more complex. While consciously acting on it in daily life, particularly in my dealings with other people, it prompted me to take a dramatic initiative when I was seventeen. I set up a youth club in Ballaghaderreen. There was nothing for the young people of the town to do that particular summer. The idea came to me. I felt God wanted me to do it, even if I did not. I was mortified at what it would entail – calling a meeting of the young people of the town and speaking in public before them. By then I was used to dealing with people through working in our pub at home, but the idea of proposing such an idea to my cynical teen peers made me want to crawl away and hide. Then I realised that if I did not do it I would be letting God down. So I called a meeting and sweated buckets as I proposed the idea to a packed attendance. We set up a committee, I was elected president, and soon we were rocking through what became one of the most exhilarating experiences of my life. We organised our own dances, opened our own shop, had walks and packed fruit to raise funds, wrote and staged our own Christmas show, and arranged bus tours, mainly to football matches.

I remember, in Christmas week of that year, going up to the local hall for a rehearsal of our show. There was a stunning sunset over Bockagh hill behind the town on that crisp, frosty afternoon in which everything was sparkling clear and defined by the cold air, even the reds of the sunset. I was overwhelmed by the beauty of it all. I thought I would burst with happiness. I wanted to get on my knees right there on the street and thank God. Instead I gazed at the setting sun and prayed my gratitude for this great life with all my heart and all my soul and all my being.

Soon the youth club involved nearly every teenager in the town, but no adults. No clergy either, though they were on every other committee in the town. Eventually I sought out a younger priest from St Nathy's and a younger nun from the convent, where we used hold our meetings, as 'advisers'. It helped keep some of the more suspicious parents happy. The priest we chose, Father Jimmy Colleran, never ever subjected any of his pupils to corporal punishment. He was also hugely into sport and started basketball at St Nathy's. And we were all in love with Sister Immaculata, who was not much older than ourselves. The youth club was a tremendous experience and all thanks to *Gaudium et Spes*, although, of its membership, only its president knew that!

By then I had been approached by two priests at St Nathy's who wondered whether I had considered the priesthood. I told them I had but did not elaborate. I was not surprised that they asked me. Sometime beforehand I was, at the request of the cathedral priests, the first lay person in the diocese to do a reading from the ambo at a Sunday Mass. It followed Vatican II liturgical reforms. So I felt the priests must have guessed that I had been thinking along such lines. But doubt had set in, and from an unexpected quarter. Celibacy was not the issue. I had little experience of sex at that age. No, my great concern was the vow of obedience. I knew myself well enough by then to be aware that I could not act against my conscience even if instructed as a priest by my bishop/religious superior. I was sufficiently aware of Catholic Church history by then too to know such could happen. It was also post-1968 and Pope Paul VI's *Humanae Vitae* encyclical, which banned artificial means of contraception. I was aware that his doing so was against the majority advice of a panel set up by the Vatican to look at the issue and, even by then, I had doubts about the Church's teachings on when human life began. I was aware how this had shifted through the millennia. I knew too that, as a priest, I could never tell a couple it was a sin for them to use contraceptives, even if that was what the Pope taught. It was not what I believed.

But, though the vow of obedience was fundamental to the growing fissures in my sense of vocation, it was not all. I was becoming troubled about some theological matters, particularly those surrounding redemption and salvation. I soon found it more and more difficult to accept that God would allow his only son die a lingering and painful death so as to expiate our sins and allow humanity's reconciliation with him. It seemed a complete contradiction of the 'God is love' teaching, making him out to be some sort of vengeful barbarian instead. It sounded primal, primitive, and was certainly remote from the divinity I had come to know. Soon I began to find that theology all too contrived and fantastic.

Later, I began to think similarly about the resurrection of Jesus. It seemed too great a claim on faith that we should be asked to believe such a thing. I loved the gospel story of the apostles on the road to Emmaus (still do!) but I was soon no longer convinced by it. After all, the Romans had records of the crucifixion of Jesus but there was nothing about his sensational resurrection except for the limited five hundred in the gospels. There was no independent verification. This too soon began to prove a mystery too far for me. I had no problem believing in Jesus or his teachings, and still don't, but his divinity would become a major issue for me. That soon evolved to include doubt about divinity itself.

But I was still at the earlier stages of such thinking while at St Nathy's. Occasionally I would bring up such questions in Christian Doctrine classes during senior years at 'the college', as it was referred to in Ballaghaderreen. But I stopped this following the reaction of our priest/teacher to my question: 'Father, how do we know that God exists?' That thoroughly decent man went into a rage. He thought I was being deliberately mischievous and provocative. I was not. I was desperately trying to find grounds to cling to a belief which had been central to my life and happiness and which was beginning to soften.

I realised from that priest's response that I had asked a question which was as absurd to him as a goldfish in a bowl asking 'How do we know that water exists?' God was that man's element and so real to him that a question as to his existence was so ridiculous as to be merely mischievous or provocative. I stopped asking questions but continued my private quest. But the more I sought satisfactory answers, the more elusive they seemed to become. God soon evolved in my mind beyond theology, beyond denomination or faith, beyond even concept. He seemed too great to be comprehended by the human mind. Human understanding of divinity, whatever the faith background, began to seem like gazing upwards through those opaque squares you see on pavements over city cellars, which admit light but no clarity. From below all you can see is amorphous movement and shadow.

In time I would feel all religions and philosophies were like peering downwards through such opaque squares at a running stream below. Each had a perspective. None had the full picture from their defined position over the dynamic flow of existence. I began to feel that nothing was really known about God, such were the limitations of the human mind in dealing with the infinite, the eternal. How could the finite conceive of the infinite?

God felt increasingly unknowable and I needed to know him to believe in him. I began to feel he was unknown and wondered how, if he was invisible, we could know he existed. I did not know. I do not know. I needed proof beyond faith. It was not forthcoming.

Such thinking took up much of my undergraduate years at university in Galway. I read widely, devouring material as I sought reassurance about the existence of God. I was also studying philosophy, which I abandoned after a year as it seemed more and more like a supermarket of ideas, each begging: 'Buy me. Believe in me.' My interest in philosophy shifted then from seeing it as part of a search for truth to locating it in its historic context, the better to establish the influence each of its many manifestations had on human affairs. I became more interested in philosophy as history. Theology began to seem increasingly headed that way too. I was so excited when I first came upon Thomas Aquinas's five proofs for the existence of God until I discovered they were proofs only for the probability of such existence. And I wasn't convinced by any of them. I waded through Teilhard de Chardin's *The Phenomenon of Man*, and a Penguin edition of St Augustine's *The City of God* through one stifling summer in New York where I was working as 'vacation relief' in an apartment complex opposite the UN building. The most helpful book I came across in those years was Hans Küng's wonderful *On Being a Christian*, but even it failed eventually to secure an ebbing faith. I was 'being lost' and knew it.

By second year at university I stopped attending Mass, as it had become meaningless, but I still continued my search for God in libraries and churches in Ireland, as well as in London and New York during the summers, but to no avail. I was a great visitor to churches in those times, part of the ongoing pursuit of my disappearing God. During the academic year I attended meetings in suburban houses in Galway, and at the university, of groups such as the US-based evangelical Campus Crusade for Christ, of the Charismatic Renewal Movement where people spoke in tongues, of believers in the Bahai religion and of the

Moonies, followers of Sun Myung Moon. There were others too. All preached abandonment to faith. All were friendly and welcoming. And all had a similar 'wipe your feet on the mat and leave your mind at the door' message. I could not leave my mind at the door. I could not believe that a God who created it would demand such a thing of me.

I soon realised I was going through a bereavement process. I missed the closeness to God that I once had. I missed above all the extraordinary dimension and depth God had added to my life, the solid assurance, the shape to this existence he had given me, the direction, the stimulus, the happiness. Without God, my spirit felt so flat at times – like a wet newspaper stuck to a damp pavement unable to lift itself whatever the effort.

I expect I went through all seven stages of grief in those years. I lost my God with deep reluctance, which is why I don't denigrate faith or believers. I know how important it can be to people and I know the price of its loss.

I moved on eventually, as one does after broken relationships. I was a very active student in Galway, whether in politics, journalism, drama, debating, or a brief attempt at mountaineering. I loved my time there. I learned to live without answers to the big questions, but with strong convictions pertaining to this life. I owe those convictions to my former belief in God and to the Catholicism which shaped me. Both left me with some of the things I most value in my life – a conscience, a strong sense of social justice, a respect for the person, compassion, deep attachment to family, friends and to community – all of which I have 'sinned' against time and again. But both also taught me how to forgive myself and start again. And to forgive others too – most of the time!

I am an agnostic, but of a strange hybrid. I am an Irish Catholic agnostic. Having lost my faith in God, I have never been able to place it to the same degree in anyone or anything else, including atheism which too requires a faith I do not have. And from experience I know there is a wisdom in religion which conveys 'truths' which can only be understood at the level of intuition. It is a level which no fundamentalist, of whatever hue, can divine. Its realm is nuance, its shades pastel, its source awe. I still feel such awe when I contemplate the vastness of this existence, its space and time, its beauty, and our humble place in all that majesty. Such sense is, of course, subjective. I allow it for myself, nonetheless. I enjoy it. All that is missing is someone to be grateful to for it all.

I do not know how this existence is here or why, but there are times when I feel uplifted by the experience of just being part of it. That helps me transcend and understand the pettiness of the moment and to appreciate that all is passing, the bad as well as the good. It allows me to hope, always. And that is the most priceless legacy of all.

Heaven on Earth – Good News to the Poor

Peter McVerry SJ

I got a lovely Christmas present this year from a young home-less man whom I have known for many years. Admittedly he was a little drunk at the time … but more about that later.

I grew up in a religious house. My father was a good doctor and a good Catholic: Sunday Mass, regular sacraments and lov-ing his neighbour. Indeed I often heard the phone ringing in the middle of the night – it was a patient who needed him and up he got, off he went and never a word of complaint. Those were the days before doctors had partners or 'practices' or locums to share the burden. It was only later I discovered that some of the callers were not even his own patients.

My mother was a nurse and a good Welsh Protestant. She met my father while working in the same hospital in England. When they decided to get married, she converted to Catholicism, to save my father from the fires of hell, which was the destiny then of any Catholic who dared to marry a Protestant. Like many converts, she became more Catholic than the Catholics themselves: family Rosary every night with all the trimmings, everyone present, no excuses accepted.

So my Catholicism, in those early days, revolved around church attendance, saying my morning and night prayers, scrupulously obeying the laws and rules and regulations de-manded by the Church – the Pharisees had nothing on me – and loving my neighbour – at least those who were deserving of being loved. Reading the Bible was a Protestant sort of thing, and we didn't do Protestant sorts of things, so my understand-ing of God, and what God desires, was entirely dependent on the words of the priests and the bishop. They were therefore up on a pedestal, representatives of God, the vehicle by which God communicated to us lesser human beings. Every Mass, every prayer, every participation in the sacraments gave me an increase in grace, and accumulating grace was the objective of life – reflecting back on it now, it was at least a slightly more noble objective, if not very different from, accumulating wealth. 'Saving my soul', through obedience to God's will as interpreted by the priests, was the ultimate priority.

One of the positive consequences of this understanding of God and religion was a strong belief in God, and a basic desire to lead a morally good life. On the other hand, it developed in me an understanding of life that was very uncomplicated: everything was simple and straightforward, the difference between good and evil (and between the good and the wicked) was very clear. God was equally uncomplicated, God's will was clear: love your neighbour, go to Mass on Sunday, no meat on Friday, and a list of other requirements. The will of God, mediated to me through the Church authorities, also developed in me a strong, but unhealthy, respect for authority, and therefore an uncritical attitude toward the *status quo*, 'the way things are'. The way society was structured was understood to be the result of the wise deliberations of those good men (it was always men) in authority, who put other people, and the common good, before themselves. It was in many ways a simple faith, an adolescent faith for that adolescent time in our lives when things are pretty black and white.

It was a young homeless fellow, called Paddy, who shattered my simple faith. As a young, enthusiastic priest who believed his job was to bring people to God, he once said to me: 'The very thought that there might be a God depresses me.' Now, Paddy was a lad whose parents were both alcoholics and he saw – and received – a lot of violence at home. He was living on the streets when I first met him, at the age of nine. He was sent to an industrial school for non-attendance at school and there he was sexually abused on many occasions, by different people in authority. In my simple faith, Paddy, as the victim of terrible suffering and abuse, must have been loved by God, a God of justice whose heart must have been torn by the sufferings of this innocent child, a God who would want to punish those responsible. Surely Paddy felt loved by this God that *I* believed in. But, no, instead he felt rejected by the God that *he* believed in.

Paddy, on release from the industrial school, began to take drugs. He used drugs to blot out the memories of the violence and abuse he had suffered in earlier childhood. When I asked him would he not think of giving up drugs, he said: 'When I stop taking drugs, I feel the pain too much.' To buy his drugs, he had to rob. He broke into people's houses, he dipped ladies' purses, he robbed from the back of cars. He was arrested and brought into Garda stations, where sometimes he got a hiding. He was sent to prison, because society thought he was bad. God suddenly became very confusing for me; right and wrong, good and evil, no longer seemed so clearcut. Paddy broke the law – and went to jail; he was assaulted by those who upheld the law – and they got promoted. Those who had abused him came from 'respectable' society; this 'respectable' society now judged him and condemned him. They wanted him out of the way because he was a problem, *their* problem. *His* problem did not seem to concern them, because nobody was doing anything about it.

I came then to realise what he meant when he said 'The very thought that there might be a God depresses me.' He felt so bad about himself, he felt that he was worthless and unlovable. Why did he think that? Because that's what everyone he knew kept telling him: parents, teachers, gardaí, sometimes even the Church. His parents showed him little love and eventually threw him out; his school expelled him because his behaviour was difficult – but his behaviour was difficult because of his problems at home; the gardaí made it clear they wanted to be rid of him; he heard the Church saying, 'robbing is bad' and he said to himself, 'I rob, so I must be bad.' The message he was getting from both the people he met and the institutions of the society he was living in was the same, 'You're no good, you're only trouble, we don't want you.' So he said to himself, 'If there is a God, then

God is up there, somewhere, looking down at me, saying: "There's someone I couldn't love, there's someone I couldn't care about"', because that was the truth about himself as he understood it – and surely God knew the truth! So he thought: 'It's bad enough going through life thinking you are unlovable, but to have to go through eternity, thinking you're unlovable – well, that's too much.' So for him, the good news was that there was no God.

What was I, a priest, to say to him about God? That God was all-loving, full of compassion, and bringing justice to our world? Such words would sound so hollow, even meaningless to him – and, I must confess, came to sound increasingly meaningless to me.

Of course, I could tell Paddy about the kingdom of God in heaven, where all will be well and God's love will be revealed. But for Paddy, that was pie in the sky, of little consolation to him in his suffering here and now, the deluded words of a brain-washed priest

And so I came to realise that you cannot *talk* to Paddy about a God who loves him, unless you first *be* the love of God to Paddy. And you cannot be the love of God to Paddy unless you try to respond concretely to the suffering and injustice which Paddy experiences every day.

Paddy cannot believe in a God who loves him, because he does not love himself. If I am to bring Paddy to God (because God is already close to Paddy), then I have to bring him to love himself – by loving him, concretely, in the here and now.

Jesus' commandment, as expressed by St John the Evangelist, was 'Love one another as I have loved you.' This always puzzled me – people don't usually get crucified by the authorities for telling everyone to love one another! Unless by love, you mean something so radical, so challenging and so threatening to the authorities and their way of life that they feel obliged to get rid of you.

Jesus was born into a society which was grossly unjust, where a small percentage of people were obscenely wealthy and the vast majority obscenely poor, many on the edge of destitution; where some were despised and unwanted and relegated to the margins of respectable society, made (like Paddy) to feel unloved by those humans amongst whom they lived, and unloved and rejected by God.

Jesus came amongst us, the revelation to us of the love of God. The poor (the likes of Paddy) flocked after him, they hung on his every word; four thousand of them spent three full days listening to him, unconcerned that they were hungry (Mark 8:2, 8); Simon Peter interrupted Jesus' night of prayer to remind him that 'everyone is looking for you' (Mark 1:37); when Jesus made to move on to other towns, 'they tried to keep him from leaving' (Luke 4:42); so many people would gather to hear him that 'Jesus and his disciples had no time to eat' (Mark 3:20); Jesus was mobbed by the poor – but the political and religious authorities, the wealthy and respectable, criticised him incessantly and plotted how to get rid of him. What on earth was going on?

The poor didn't search Jesus out and listen to him for hours on end because he was offering them a place in the kingdom of God in heaven, because he was telling them that all will be well when finally they depart this world. No, Jesus was offering them a more concrete hope and expectation: hope, here and now, in the midst of their miserable existence, and the expectation of a better life, here and now (as also, of course, in the life to come). The kingdom of God that Jesus preached was not just a distant dream that belonged to a different world and another time; no, the kingdom of God was at hand.

> Now after John was arrested, Jesus came to Galilee, proclaiming the Good News of God, and saying, 'The time is fulfilled, and the kingdom of God has come near; repent, and believe in the Good News' (Mark 1:14-15).

This kingdom belonged to the poor:

> Happy are you who are poor: yours is the kingdom of God.
> Happy are you who are hungry now: you will be filled.
> Happy are you who weep now: you will laugh'[5] (Luke 6:20-21).

---

5. Weep, from the poverty in which they and their families live.

29

But for the rich and powerful, things were also going to be turned upside down in the kingdom of God:

> But woe to you who are rich, for you have received your con-
> solation.
> Woe to you who are full now, for you will be hungry.
> Woe to you who are laughing now, for you will mourn and
> weep (Luke 6:24-26).

What was this kingdom that Jesus preached, so attractive to the poor but so threatening to the rich and powerful? In the prayer that Jesus gave to the early Christian community, Jesus declared his mission and invited the early Church to join in that mission and prayed that that it might succeed:

> Thy kingdom come (or, in other words, 'Thy will be done')
> on earth as it is in heaven (Matthew 6:10).

Jesus came to replicate on earth the kingdom of God in heaven
In the kingdom of God in heaven, everyone's needs will be met, everyone will be equal and respected and loved, no one will feel rejected or unwanted or looked down upon.

In the kingdom of God on earth, Jesus promised that everyone's needs, too, will be met, everyone will be equal and respected and loved, no-one will feel rejected or unwanted or looked down upon.

How on earth (literally) did Jesus intend to replicate the kingdom of God in heaven? Through the new community that Jesus was initiating, a community of disciples – which today we call the Christian community – whose lives together here on earth would reflect that kingdom of God in heaven. And so Jesus' vision was that the kingdom of God in heaven, where God's will is always done, would be replicated in this new community on earth that he was establishing.

It appears that Jesus expected this new community to be a community of poor people. Why? In a community of equality, respect and service of each other, the needs of the poor would be met; the relationships that characterised the community would ensure that the poor would not go hungry and, where they had fallen into debt to feed their families, their debts would be forgiven.

> Give us this day our daily bread,and forgive us our debts as we forgive those who are indebted to us (Matthew 6:11-12).

This was not a prayer that the rich could say: their larders were full. It was a prayer only the poor could say. The same Jesus who promised, 'Ask and you shall receive' was now promising the poor that their prayer for food for the day and forgiveness of past debts would be fulfilled. How was Jesus going to fulfil this promise?

The prayer of the poor would be heard – through the community
This new community, which was to resemble the kingdom of God in heaven, was Good News to the poor and to those who were willing to live a life of service, in solidarity and equality with the poor. Those who were better-off and in positions of power and authority would simply not be interested in it. Indeed they would resent it, and persecute it, as it would not afford them the recognition and status they felt they deserved, and it would make demands on their resources which they would not be willing to accept.

The equality that characterises the kingdom of God, both on earth and in heaven, occurs in the Incarnation itself. God came to the people of God, not by identifying with a religious leader, or a powerful prince, or with someone in authority but by identifying with a crucified victim of religious and political oppression. This crucified victim, the least in the kingdom of Caesar, is leader and king, the first in the kingdom of God.

This new community, then, represents, in history, what God desires for all humanity in the face of poverty and oppression – a community which lives together in solidarity and equality, and so in justice and peace, over whom God, through Jesus, can reign. In such a community, poverty and exclusion have been abolished. The hope and salvation of all humanity are to be found in this community.

This community, where the needs of all would be met, and all would enjoy equal status, is not some socialist utopia. The leader of this Christian community is the Risen Jesus himself. Those who choose to follow the Risen Jesus do precisely that: they follow the One who gave everything he had, everything he was, even what was most precious to him, life itself, for the sake of his brothers and sisters. In sharing all that we have, all that we are, even what is most precious to us, we are simply following his commandment, a radical, challenging commandment: 'Love one another as I have loved you.' A commandment that threatens our securities, our comfort zones, our sense of what constitutes a normal life.

This community, with Jesus as its king, is the reign of God in history
The Christian community – local parish communities as well as the worldwide Christian community – is, then, intended to be a witness to that community of equality and respect that is the kingdom of God in heaven. Entry to this community is for those who wish to affirm, in their own relationships with others, the equality and dignity of everyone, especially the poor, and thereby commit themselves to ensuring that the needs of all, especially the poor, are fulfilled. That is what Jesus did in his own life and, therefore, what he calls his followers to do. The Christian community must be judged then, not by the quantity of its membership, but by the quality of its witness.

And so to my Christmas present
On Christmas day, this young man rang me – having earlier, of course, texted me, looking for credit for his phone! – and asked me 'What did God give you as a present on his birthday?'

I said: 'He gave me nothing, I haven't had a present all day.'

I went on: 'And what did God give you?' I asked, 'Nothing, as well, I suppose?'

'No', he said, 'I got a present from God, God gave me you.'

And in that sentence, this drunken young homeless man expressed what it means to be a Christian far better than all the theologians in the world.

On Being a Catholic

Nuala O'Loan

I have often given thanks for my faith – without it the world would be a different place. It informs every moment of every day. It is at the core of my being for I know that, strange and mysterious as it has seemed to me on so many occasions, God made me and I belong to him.

I have observed that during our lives each of us will play many roles. I am currently wife, mother, daughter, sister, cousin, friend, former Police Ombudsman, etc. In the midst of all that those different roles entail, it can be hard to remain focused on why I am here and on what God calls me to do, what his purpose is for me in life; what being a Catholic really means for me.

I learned as a little girl why God made me: to know him, to love him and to serve him in this world and to be happy with him for ever in the next; that I should love him with all my heart and all my soul, and should love others as he has loved me, without qualification. As a little girl it was really quite simple – I remember, aged about five years, sitting in a row of little girls learning the words of the Christmas carol, 'Little Jesus sweetly sleep, do not stir, we will lend a coat of fur. We will rock you, rock you, rock you, we will serve you all we can, darling, darling little man.' As we sang we cradled our arms to hold the baby Jesus. We understood the baby Jesus – we knew the beauty of the little child and we loved him.

Later I learned of God. He sat on a cloud in a long white robe, in a picture on the back of Sr Veronica's classroom door, knowing all that we did and thought – a rather remote frightening being. Through liturgy and music, I learned to worship. I learned to pray, and that through prayer I would be nourished and strengthened and I would be safe, knowing that indeed he is God and he does carry me in the palm of his hand. I made May altars for Our Lady with bluebells in jam jars, and I learned to call into the church and light a candle and say a prayer, especially when life was difficult – a habit which has sustained me all my life in many different parts of the world. I learned of the sacraments of the church – those sources of life and nourishment and healing.

One of the wonderful things about being a Catholic for me has been that ability to go to church anywhere in the world, even where I do not speak the language of the people, and to know what is happening, to participate in the liturgy and to know that I belong.

Being a Catholic is being part of what should be a praying, worshipping, caring community. The response which we get when we reach out or when we offer help is part of our experience of Church, part of our living of the mystery of life. On some occasions the response is negative. For some, like some of the children of the industrial schools, or the mothers who were sent to the Magdalen laundries, it was terribly negative. That response was nothing to do with the teaching of Jesus. It was something which shames us all – something which was known by so many, but which was not dealt with.

There have been other episodes in the life of the Catholic Church – the torture of the Inquisition, the burning of people who would not become Catholic – shameful, criminal activities which are part of our history, and which we must remember as we remember the human fallibility of the church in so many matters such as the work of Galileo, the process of 'churching' women after childbirth, the attitudes towards sexuality, the distancing of the hierarchy from the people of God, the failures by some in our Church to act fairly on those occasions on which false allegations of abuse were made against priests and religious. Similar failings can be found in other churches too. The lesson to be learned is that we must be cautious and watchful for abuse in all its forms. As Lord Acton famously said: 'Everything secret degenerates, even the administration of justice, nothing is safe that does not show how it can bear discussion and publicity.' As members of the Church we must ensure that we see Christ in all whom we meet, and to answer the call of Micah, which I first heard when I was eighteen, that 'This is what the Lord asks of you: that you act justly, love tenderly and walk humbly with your God' (Micah 6:8).

So it is that the most important thing to me about being a Catholic is that I am called to holiness, to a relationship with God which is to me eternally unfathomable, and yet eternally real. The words of the psalmist, 'Let me see your face O Lord, hide not your face', are a very real prayer. I seek to know God and yet each time I think that I do know him, I know that it cannot be him, because if I understand him, then I have in some way reduced his divinity to fit my human understanding, and in so doing I have not understood and I do not know him. As the years have passed I have come to a much deeper understanding, an understanding which has continued to grow all my life – but which has, on occasion, seemed to desert me, leaving me unable to find the God whom I seek, unable to know him. I have learned through the years that the times of darkness come to an end. There are moments, too, when his presence is so strong that there is great joy in the knowledge of his being, and of this relationship with the infinitely mysterious which I can never understand, but which inspires, enables and informs every day of my life.

This call to holiness is undoubtedly a most significant call. I believe that it demands of each of us that we do not live lives of mediocrity; that we live our lives using our skills and talents in the service of him who made us. In his book, *Costing not less than Everything*, John Dalrymple talks about how Jesus is our role model: how we can see how he lived, how he divided up his time, how he reacted to people when they made demands of him, wanting to be cured of illness, wanting him to bring back to life those who had died, wanting him to tell them how to live their lives. His teaching is preserved for us in the gospels.

Reading them, we will become aware of how he repeatedly went away from those who were with him, to pray. We know that he talked about his Father's business. We know what that business was. We have seen that his love for us was a love which expressed itself in total giving and total submission to the will of God. I know that this is what I should be prepared for.

To a certain extent it can be frustrating to be a woman in the Church. So many of the opportunities for service are available only to men. Many women have the capacity and desire to make a greater contribution and yet this is denied to them. The church would undoubtedly be enriched if the voice of women were heard more frequently across the whole range of issues. I have no doubt that this will change. I know also that in so many ways the call to holiness is not easy, but that does not matter, for we do not do what we are called to do alone. We do it with the help of the God who made us. As St Paul says in his letter to the Philippians: 'I can do all things in the power of him who saved me' (Philippians 4:13). Sometimes these seem to me to be almost arrogant claims. It can seem that to think that like this is to assume to oneself something of the power of God. But actually, I have observed that to live out the call to holiness is to live in humility and love.

There have been absolutely wonderful moments in my life which I cherish, and which were so very special. My most sacred moments have included the births of our five sons. Giving birth was a time when I always felt that I was engaged in an elemental struggle, the struggle for life, and that God was there in all his strength holding me, being with me. That moment when the monumental struggle to give birth is over, when the pain recedes and one looks in awe on the face of a newborn child, is a very special time. We are much blessed in our five sons.

There have been moments, too, when I have felt the stillness and have known that I am in the presence of God. Some of those moments were very simple – the silence of watching the new dawn on a glorious day as the sun rises, the greening of a lovely tree as the spring advances, the opening of a very special flower such as the wonderful white flower which blossoms during the night, for one night only, in Kenya. They call it the Queen of the Night. In the morning it is dying, but for a brief period it is exquisitely beautiful. I have wondered why it flowers in such glory for only one night.

As an eighteen year old at school I encountered the poet Hopkins who wrote that

> The world is charged with the grandeur of God
> It will flame out, like shining from shook foil
> It gathers to greatness like the ooze of oil
> Crushed.

I have seen this grandeur on so many occasions and have marvelled at the magnificence of the creation of our world.

There is another reality, however. The reality of earthquakes, tsunamis, famine, terrorism – times when life can seem impossible, and the world can seem very cruel. There is also the less globally dramatic reality of terminal sickness which comes too early, of suicide, of deep anger and despair. Much of this is to some degree incomprehensible. We all encounter, in some measure, loss and bereavement, loneliness and disappointment, frustration and even hopelessness. At these times I have found that being a Catholic sustains me – that even when I cannot pray, the act of being in a church while others pray has made it possible for me to carry on. In the darkest times I have sat in an empty darkened church and gazed on the crucified Christ and in his suffering I have come to some strange dark comfort, some cloudy understanding that he, who is the Son of God, suffered so terribly that he cried out in agony, 'My God, My God why have you forsaken me?' In such darkness the light has gently dawned and I have gone back to life heartened.

Hopkins talks of the darkness that can be life but concludes his poem:

> And for all this, nature is never spent;
> There loves the dearest freshness deep down things ...
> Because the Holy Ghost over the bent
> World broods with warm breast and with ah! bright wings.

St Patrick in his great prayer talks of the journey through life and of the presence and power of Christ in our lives. He concludes:

Christ in hearts of all that love me,
Christ in mouth of friend and stranger.

In these words lies the challenge to see the face of Christ in all whom I meet and in all those whose lives touch my life. It is not hard to see the face of Christ in a new-born child, in a dearly loved old person, in those in whom goodness is almost palpable. It is not easy to see the face of Christ in someone who has done terrible things and the challenge I have found is to be able to go behind what has happened and to try and understand. When I was pregnant and lost our first baby after being caught in a bomb explosion, I could not understand the evil that planted the bomb which took our baby's life. I sought over many years to comprehend and to forgive. As with so many of life's trials I eventually learned to leave the issue for God, knowing that I had not walked in the shoes of those who planted the bomb and I would never understand, and that perhaps the most important thing was that my lost child was safe, safe in Christ's cradling.

Cardinal Bernardin wrote, in *The Gift of Peace*, of the call to love and of what it will demand of us:

As Christians, if we are to love as Jesus loved, we must first come to terms with suffering. Like Jesus, we simply cannot be cool and detached from our fellow human beings. Our years of living as Christians will be years of suffering for and with other people. Like Jesus, we will love others only if we walk with them in the valley of darkness – the dark valley of sickness, the dark valley of moral dilemmas, the dark valley of oppressive structures and diminished rights.

Those words have seemed very relevant in Northern Ireland over the years. I sat as a counsellor for many years with people in distress, as they sought to understand what had happened and to work out a way forward in the face of what was on occasion horrendous suffering, much of it relating to 'The Troubles', as we euphemistically refer to our forty years of terrorism, death and destruction. When I was Police Ombudsman, I sat with many people who were in great pain, sometimes decades after an event, as they told the stories of murder and mayhem. They told me of their suspicions and their fears that police officers had either participated in murder, allowed it to happen or did not investigate it after it happened. My professional work involved investigating these terrible cases and telling what was to be told faithfully, not hiding that which might be unacceptable. People have the right to know if a police officer was wrongly accused, and equally he or she had the right for the fact that there was no basis to the accusation to be made known. If the police had failed or there had been collusion it was important to articulate that too. One of the great tenets of our faith is the articulation of truth and the belief, as St John recorded, that 'The truth will set you free.'

One of the most humbling aspects of my work as Police Ombudsman was the number of times I encountered the determination not to allow a terrible crime, which had destroyed a family unit by taking one of its members, to destroy the unity and goodness of that family.

I have learned too that for all of us there will be times when we are the consoler, and times when we need to be consoled, times when we rely on others to walk with us sustaining us in our difficulties and times when we must offer that same comfort to others, and above all this, and around all this and in all this is 'the love of God made visible in Christ Jesus our Lord.'

As St Augustine said:

You have made us for yourself O Lord
And our hearts are restless until they find rest in you.

Being Catholic: Catholic Being

Mary T. Malone

Last August at 3.00am on the morning of my seventieth birthday, I was jolted awake by my bedside phone. I knew immediately whose voice I would hear at the other end of the transatlantic line – that of my closest Canadian friend, Shirley, who was days from death in the palliative care unit of a Toronto hospital. A short time earlier I had spent a week with her in that same hospital, and with much laughter, shared reminiscences, and not a few tears, we had said our goodbyes in person. One day I had brought Communion from her convent where I was staying, and on a gorgeous summer's day, we had shared our last Eucharist together in the hospital roof garden. Now on this August morning, as I took a deep breath before answering, I knew that this was going to be one of the most important phone conversations of my life. Everything in my seventy-year life of being Catholic and Catholic being had to come to focus in that one moment.

Her breath was ragged and I knew someone was helping her with the phone and oxygen mask. After the birthday greetings, we asked in turn the usual opening question of our most heartfelt conversations, 'What is in you heart at this moment?' She could speak only in monosyllables, but that seemed the most appropriate form of communication and nothing else was needed: home, memory, life, death, fullness and emptiness, gratitude and longing, and, above all else, friendship and love. We had been friends for forty-four years and that breath-taking conversation summed it all up. Shirley died a few days later and her life was celebrated with joy and grief by her religious community. I have since then visited her grave for yet another form of goodbye.

What were the steps on my Catholic journey that had

brought me to this place? I was a cradle Catholic, born the third child and first girl of a family of eight, in a small north Wexford village at a time when babies just a few hours old were rushed to the church to be christened. (The word baptism was not an active part of our vocabulary at that time.) Twelve years later my first conscious act of Catholic rebellion took place when, against the wishes of the attending mid-wife, the whole family gathered around the parental bed to kiss the new and final arrival. 'The devil', we were told, 'had not yet been removed.' Several days later I accompanied my mother at her churching and was covered with a blushing confusion as I half-heard and half-understood what was so furtively going on. Apart from that, the routine Irish Catholic life of the 1940s and 1950s was simply part of the air we breathed, something I now realise that was much larger and more profound than the daily Masses and family Rosaries, the weekly confessions, the seasonal devotions, the annual Ferns catechism examination (I was a whiz!), and the novenas, benedictions, medals, scapulars, annual mission and Corpus Christi processions in the nearby town that marked the Catholic year. We sang the *Tantum Ergo* and *Stabat Mater* with gusto, and even though this was not required of girls, we all knew the Latin Mass responses, as well as our altar-boy brothers.

At the time there was little reflection on any of this, except for the ongoing underground murmur about the priest asking for money again. Sermons happened, but were entirely unremarkable, and not expected to be anything else. The annual mission priests 'gave out' about the usual sins, but once they had gone, we all returned to the normal routines of village life.

Now as I search my memories, I can recall the spasmodic cruelty of one of the priests, but little else that disturbed what was, for the most part, a happy and carefree existence. There was a kind of informal and unofficial system of community welfare and shoes and clothes did the rounds and food was shared so that no one was destitute and no one was homeless. It was by no means an ideal way of life, but the simple fact that everyone knew everyone else, and almost everything *about* everyone else, exercised a kind of behaviour control, and kept us from the worst excesses. I never felt other than safe and experienced a sense of belonging in family, church and village, that I now realise has marked my Catholic life in significant ways.

I did not know then that my departure for boarding school at the age of thirteen closed many of these doors, if only because of physical absence from home and village for most of the year. Convent boarding school made somewhat explicit what had been implicit in my Catholic upbringing till then. The nuns were concerned about our lives and set specific standards of behaviour and religious practice that sometimes seemed laughable. Our Catholic life became more intensive and, to some extent, more expressive. For me, church music played a large part in this, as well as the obvious care taken to surround the liturgy with beauty and solemnity. I felt a deepening of a spiritual life that I was just becoming aware of. We became proficient in plain chant and polyphony, as well as in some occasionally sentimental but much loved seasonal hymns. My repertoire of Catholicity was expanding, at least in the experiential sense. We had religion classes and religion exams, but these were regarded as challenges to rote learning rather than invitations to mature reflection. Almost every year it was announced that some senior girls were entering the convent, and in January 1957 four of us Wexford girls left for England to do precisely that. From the vantage point of my seventy years, I am overwhelmed at this decision to leave my family and my home and my country, fully assuming that I would never see them again. Now I know what a momentous break this was, but at the time, I did not experience the searing sense of loss that I have since discovered at the core of my being. I never saw my father again, nor was I allowed to attend his funeral – that was fairly routine custom in the religious life of the 1950s.

Catholic life in the convent boarding school had been an extension of family life and, in many ways, convent life in the 1950s just carried on the tradition, more or less as it had for centuries. It all seemed such a natural development, and even the experience of three thirty-day Ignatian retreats in the space of eight years, while again expanding my Catholic repertoire, did not radically disturb the even tenor of my spiritual life.

But changes were on the horizon. In 1958, Pope Pius XII died, and for the first time in my life I watched television for his funeral. Tears of awe streamed down my novice's face as I watched the Roman Catholic Church in action, with its streams of bishops from all over the world. For the next few years these television events seemed to occur with regularity as popes came and went and, most important of all for my Catholic being, the Second Vatican Council started its momentous task in 1962.

In the early 1960s, I was sent to Canada by my religious community for doctoral studies at the University of Toronto, and it seems now that the moment my feet touched down on Canadian soil, my Catholic life changed irrevocably. These were the 'interesting times' of the old proverb, and I can just list some of the strands that fed into the recreation of my Catholic being on the rich soil of my Catholic past.

Since the kind of theological studies that I wished were not then available to me as a woman, I started on the study of early Christian patristic literature in Greek and Latin through the Department of Classics, without at all being aware that ressourcement was going to be one of the central tenets of post-conciliar life. My main focus was the study of Christian attitudes to women in the early Church, a life-long personal and professional study, which continues with even more urgency. Canada took to the Council with enthusiasm and as each document emerged, vast discussions produced even vaster excitement. The feminist Christian movement was burgeoning and I joined a campus-based group that was focused on the restoration of the female diaconate, for which my research provided some of the 'ammunition'. Religious Life was also changing in dramatic ways, for me inspired not only by conciliar documents, but also by what I was reading in Augustine, Ambrose, Jerome, Chrysostom and others. The 1960s campaigns for civil rights and the anti-war movements led me into life-altering contact with groups of Catholic and later Mennonite pacifists. Liturgical life was changing, and eventually theological study was more freely available to all. By then, in the early 1970s, I was teaching patristic theology and Church history in the archdiocesan seminary, and discovered my true vocation as a Catholic educator.

My departure from convent life after seventeen years was not nearly as momentous as some of the literature might indicate. I remained and still remain on the closest terms with my former community and, through my studies, developed a huge admiration for women's religious life through the ages. Without the continuing witness of these women, the history of Catholic women would be almost entirely absent from the annals of Christianity.

All my life, from the earliest sibling rivalry with my brothers, the question 'Where are the women?' had haunted me. Now, that was the question that came into clearer and more urgent historical and theological focus. The question of women in the Church was being raised in several contexts. Bishops studying the development of lay ministry were asking it in ecclesiastical contexts. Women studying theology, after initial enthusiasm, were wondering why mainstream generic theology sounded so alien to their spiritual lives. Church historians were asking it as they discovered the forgotten story of women Christians. This was an exhilarating time for me as a woman Catholic. I seemed to be in the midst of the action, and part of a Catholic Church that was vibrant. Before the end of my studies I had begun working as a member of a team in a Toronto parish. Here I discovered another level of communication, as the parishioners were invited into scripture study, new liturgical experiences, and what was simply called the 'New Catechetics' for both children and adults. As I journeyed between seminary, theology college and parish, my Catholic horizons seemed to expand exponentially, and eventually I travelled across North America lecturing in universities, schools and parishes, both in Catholic and ecumenical circles, with an ease that now astonishes me. My all too brief marriage opened new Catholic doors, especially as I accompanied my husband, Michael, through a debilitating illness, with brilliant discussion about the mystery of life and death.

And then I lost my Catholic voice, and engaged in a kind of personal excommunication. In the midst of the reciprocal process that all education, but particularly theological and cate-chetical education, is, I had always been able to look people, women and men in the eye, with the assurance that I could put my full integrity behind what I was saying. The gift of a histori-cal background was one of the greatest benefits to me. It lent space and opportunity to trace developments both in structure and understanding. As Bernard Lonergan said, 'Concepts have dates.' There was a time and a place and a reason for such devel-opments, and all this provided a basis for the hope that the pat-tern would continue. But it began to be apparent that one set of dates was being chosen as the definitive moment for under-standing everything about the Catholic Church and, for many in officialdom, this was not necessarily the scriptural date, but one hovering around the Tridentine moment.

Besides, a deeply felt need was emerging in me to pray and speak in my own voice from the depth of my own experience as a woman. *Fides quaerens intellectum*, 'faith seeking understand-ing', that old quasi definition of doing theology, raised the ques-tions of *whose* faith, *who* was doing the seeking and *whose* mean-ing was being established. Having familiarised myself with what had emerged from male reflection on male experience and male faith, I now needed to know what women had contributed. I realised that the Christian tradition, as I knew it, was only a partial representation of the totality of Christian riches. So I went back to the beginning and began to explore matristic theo-logy, which, since the silencing of women in the early decades of Christianity, presented me with an almost impossible task. Hand in hand with the historical search, I set out intentionally to reconfigure the symbolic religious furniture of my mind. Prayer, both public and private, had become impossible for me. I was deeply involved, at many levels, in movements for the ordination of women, but I now grasped that the priesthood was a male construct, designed, experienced, celebrated, ritualised and theologised by men. This was a fact of history, and even though I had had my angry feminist moments around the issue of women's priestly ordination, this was not one of those moments. It was more a moment of gradually claiming as reality something that I had known all my life. I have absolutely no doubt whatever that women have to be fully included at every level in the reality of the Catholic Church, but the shape of that involvement needs to be in historical continuity with our past as women believers.

About twenty years ago, I set out to immerse myself in the one coherent body of women's theological writing in the Catholic tradition, namely the writings of the medieval women mystics, from about 1150-1450. And here I am beginning to rediscover my voice and my prayer and my God, all as fully a part of the Catholic tradition as my old patristic friends. My God has now been freed into a mystery beyond maleness and femaleness. It seems that I spent the first half of my life capturing God in dogma and symbol, and the second half freeing God to be God, and thereby freeing myself. Augustine comes to my help – *si comprehendis non est deus* – which more or less means that if we think we know who God is, then what we know is not God.

I have also been searching the tradition for the words of mothers, particularly for any sign at all that the tradition contains the Christian reflection of even one woman on the experience of conceiving, carrying, delivering and nurturing a child. I am still searching and appreciate ever more deeply what a loss this is to Catholic being.

So being Catholic and Catholic being means for me now the acceptance of a whole tradition, where I have been, in a sense, part of a diaspora of women. I am discovering a new love for the possible whole tradition, where the theological and spiritual lives of women will be as valuable as that of men. I can now weave in and out of both worlds: the mainstream generic world of traditional history, theology and Catholic life, and the tiny new shoots of what I have come to call 'Woman Christianity'. The dots are joining up, and the major excitement of medieval mystics about the mysterious and extravagant availability of God in creation, Eucharist, and compassionate community, is beginning to take hold. I feel that I have rediscovered my Catholic integrity, that I can look down the ages and, though not trivialising the often appalling treatment of women through two millennia, can see that Catholic being will not survive fully into the next millennium, without the benefit of women's participation at the heart of Catholic being.

A Church of the Streets

Aidan Troy

The journey of my life has had many twists and turns. It started in Bray, Co. Wicklow over sixty years ago and this chapter is being written in Paris. The journey in between still surprises me and, who knows, there may be a few more twists to come.

I see the course of a person's life as not just accidental but following a plan that God has laid out for each of his people. Each person and generation is on a type of Exodus journey like the people of old. We leave and we look to get somewhere else. My life started in a Catholic family with rock solid faith and practice. This was reinforced by convent and religious brothers schools attended. Finishing secondary school towards the mid-1960s, I, like so many of that generation, had no idea of what lay just around the corner for the world and the Church. In the mid 1980s, while studying in San Francisco, an ex-Chief of Police from the 1960s told of just how little he and his colleagues understood, never mind appreciated, the 'flower power' and 'make love, not war' generation that would become a feature of that beautiful city.

When I entered a novitiate the Second Vatican Council (1962-1965) was well under way. There were whispers of something stirring in the Church. But the message of the novitiate was of continuity with the past rather than any sense of embracing a new future. Forming future religious and priests was carried out according to models of life already set out and handed down from generation to generation. Even then I wondered about this, but such doubts were explained as temptations of the Devil that should be avoided at all costs.

It surprised me, for instance, that because I came from a seaside resort and attended the minor seminary, unlike most of my class from a young age, I was regarded with some suspicion. It seemed that the novitiate's role was to straighten me out and undo most of what had been achieved by my family upbringing and values. It was extraordinary to listen to words such as, 'the world', 'pop music', 'discos', 'girls', 'certain sports', 'temptations of the flesh', 'custody of the eyes' – to mention just a few – that were always used in a negative and foreboding way.

My mother died six months into my novitiate year. There was no contact with family except a letter at Christmas or on a special occasion. My mother's death was beyond anything I had imagined happening and made me wonder about this God whom I wanted to serve as a religious and priest. Strange sort of God by any standards! This first shock of my adult life left me with a stark choice – either to stay in the novitiate out of personal conviction or to leave because I was there to please someone else. That call to honest motivation in making decisions has stood to me down the years.

The novitiate year ended with the profession of vows and re-entry into 'the world'. The challenge in university of philosophical debate and the excitement of discussion was so refreshing. This contrasted sharply with the life back in the monastery which was truthfully 'another world', one that held on to past practices that no longer had meaning for the vast majority of students then seeking to engage with the Church in the modern world.

There was a real dichotomy between the world of studies outside and inside the monastery. In this form of religious life conformity to rules and regulations took precedence over honest talk. To express opinions within the religious community was not encouraged. This was a breeding ground for cover-up, something that is still painfully evident in recent reports of child abuse by religious and clergy.

After eight years of formal studies and training to be a priest I was surprised at how happy and relaxed I became. During my student days I had been on medication to help me to sleep and for 'nerves', as it was then termed. From the day I left student formation until today I have never taken more than an aspirin or antibiotic. Whatever the merits or otherwise of my training, it is doubtful if anything could have prepared me for what lay ahead.

Looking back over the past forty-five years as a religious and almost forty as a priest, I am so grateful for what God has sent my way. What a great life among his people has been mine! It would bore you, dear reader, if I gave you dates, places, times, apostolates and all that has made my life since then. I will spare you most of that.

After over twenty years preaching and in administration, in the mid 1990s I began six years in Rome as part of the central government of the Passionists. Being able to travel to many countries around the world, I saw something of the wonderful diversity of what it can mean to be Catholic. I saw the wonders of God at work among people of different cultures and situations. This marvellous diversity taught me not to worry too much about the 'footnotes' of being Catholic and risk missing the bigger text. It saddens me to find that sometimes the guardians of the footnotes seem more appreciated than the readers and interpreters of the text. When Jesus was teaching in the synagogue, 'his teaching made a deep impression on them because, unlike the scribes, he taught them with authority' (Mark 1:22).

I hope what I am going to write next does not sound proud or bumptious. When it seemed to me that nothing very new or exciting was likely to happen at this stage of my life, God gifted me the best seven years of my life as a religious and a priest. It happened like this. At the end of my six years in Rome I enrolled for one year of study at university in Rome to give me time to consider the next step. This is how I have tried to find the will of God. My provincial superior took the burden of deciding off me when he asked me to go to Belfast as local superior of a community and to become a parish priest. I had never been a parish priest before, not even a curate. Learning at this stage of my life about parish administration, schools, hospitals, etc. really scared me. I asked the provincial for one exemption – that I be excused from having anything to do with schools or their management. I suspect that he was so glad to get my agreement that he would have agreed to anything within reason. This happened in November 2000 while I was studying in Rome.

In June 2001, while packing and prior to saying a fond farewell to Rome, I spotted on the internet that there had been some disturbance at a North Belfast school. To my shock I saw that it was in Holy Cross Parish where I was due to become parish priest that August. Being an optimist, I believed all would be resolved long before I got there.

Some may know that far from being resolved the return to school on the 3 September 2001 began a three month obscenity, as young girls were harassed and abused on their way to and from primary school. On that first morning a group of parents asked if I would walk with them along the road to school which they had not used from mid-June onwards. Their opinion was I might turn out to be some form of insurance for them. Little did I know that this would begin a chapter in my life that would change me beyond anything that had happened to me before.

Now I began to realise why, when asked about the kingdom, Christ had placed a child in the centre as the model and made it clear that unless we change and become like little children we will not enter that kingdom. During those three months I saw the forgiveness in the eyes of children even when they were being terrorised. At the end of the whole sorry affair, I never once heard a child say a hateful word. One pupil, when asked did she hate the people who had blocked her way to school, answered that she didn't – she simply wanted to know why they hated her and her friends so much. At the end of the first week of the school protest, one little girl came along and tugged my sleeve and gave me a little packet of sweets. Foolishly I thanked her mother who stood beside her, only to be told that it was her daughter who had suggested this and bought the sweets with her own money to say thanks. That brings the kingdom very close.

Those months made me reflect daily on what being Catholic meant for us all. Was it a sectarian badge or was it a call to understanding, dialogue and, ultimately, forgiveness? It had to be the latter. When I recalled my November 2000 request not to have anything to do with schools, I realised what a sense of humour God has when he leads us to places we would prefer not to go. He also brings forward people of all ages and outlooks who show qualities that are not immediately obvious.

A revelation to me during those days was seeing a real living 'church of the streets'. This, when it exists, is so powerful. Walking each day for three months to and from school brought me closer to the people of the parish than I could ever have imagined. I did nothing for these people other than stand firmly with them and on occasion carry death threats and personal abuse because of my association with them and their children. Their trust in me after less than a month in the parish was humbling. Without me realising it at the time, I was becoming a religious and a priest such as I had never been before. God, through this situation and these people, was changing me radically and for the better. For allowing me to see the traces of the kingdom during those days and since, I could not thank God and these people enough.

Then when I thought I could begin learning how to become a parish priest, something happened that again touched families and the whole community so deeply. It started in April 2003 when a great young man of seventeen years hanged himself in the monastery garden just beside the church. It was awful. He was so young and so loved and his death altered his family and the whole community.

As had happened at the school blockade, I hadn't a clue what to do. But the people from the church of the streets rallied round and together we saw through as best we could the young man's funeral and a mobilisation of people to tackle the scourge of suicide. But worse was to come.

From the end of 2003 and into 2004, suicides increased to double figures in three months. We were thrown back into searching together how to deal with this appalling loss of young life and to support those who were broken by their losses. For my part, there was little I could offer other than to stand solid with the community and be present in their time of need. Those families were nothing short of heroic. Suicide is no respecter of religious or political allegiance and soon it became clear from colleagues of different churches that we had these tragedies in common. Soon I found that doors in homes and halls were open to me in connection with suicide that might not have been so following the school blockade. The Catholic dimension wasn't sectarian, but inclusive. It is not that suicide is good for this reason, but tears and loss are not Catholic or Protestant, but deeply human.

It is so important never to 'use' events like these to make religious or personal capital. It is my belief that to be Catholic means being deeply human and being ready to stand alongside the broken-hearted. When I was eighteen and left Bray, I joined the Passionist Congregation that seeks to make a link between the Crucified Christ and the crucified of the world. The main way I tried to be faithful to this calling was by preaching the word. This I did faithfully for thirty years all over Ireland and further afield. It is up to others to assess what, if anything, I have achieved.

In my heart of hearts I know that what I accomplished was very little because I did not yet know the extent of the power of the cross to release strength and generosity among God's people. When their children are under threat or their families are broken by suicide, the power of God breaks through powerfully. Just as I will never forget my mother's sudden death when I was in the novitiate, or my father's during the Holy Cross protest, people have shown me the depth of the cross and the power of the resurrection. In that sense I can truthfully say that it is these people who have taught me most effectively what being Catholic means. It is beyond belief what they gave to me and what they mean to me.

Being Catholic now means waiting to see where the next

twist in the road will lead. It so often comes unexpectedly. I will die grateful to so many people whom God has allowed into my life and who have helped me to love God as I now do.

The most recent twist in the road has been painful. The move away from those people, who formed me into being more genuinely Catholic, has left me broken-hearted. After seven years sharing the church of the streets I simply wanted to live and love those most extraordinary people for whatever years God has planned for me. No longer did I want to be their parish priest but rather their friend and fellow traveller. It wasn't to be. These people were never going to succeed in having that decision reversed. Maybe they wanted to offer thanks in the deepest sense of Eucharist. I wonder if something new is stirring that sooner or later will affect what being Catholic means to me?

CHAPTER SIX

Parish Football and the Catholic Faith

Seán Kelly

My father and his father before him were Catholics, so were their grandparents and great grandparents and everything I say about my father's people applies to my mother's people as well. That's the way it was in our community of Kilcummin, which is situated just a few miles outside Killarney, where I grew up.

Everybody in our parish was Catholic, or so it seemed to us. Protestants, Presbyterians, dissenters and agnostics were people who lived far, far away. Thus, Catholicism was the natural order. Our lives revolved around it. All the great feasts of the Church were celebrated with reverence. The sacraments were seriously observed and, yes, keeping holy the Sabbath was sacrosanct. The Lord rested on the seventh day – thank God for that! And so did everybody else. The manual labour of the farm ceased on Sundays and Holy Days. That mantra applied to us. It applied to everybody in Kilcummin. And it was most welcome. Imagine, only for our Lord we would have to work everyday. The parish priest held sway in the parish. The Stations were big events and only the best of men dined with him after Mass. Thus I never got to hear what they discussed at table – I didn't make the grade. Occasionally there would be a murmuring of discontent. One revolved around our other great passion – football.

Kilcummin rarely won anything on the playing fields but then one day they won an under-age competition – our first trophy in years. The trouble was we had a 'banger' on board. A 'banger' is the name given for an illegal player. Truth to tell in those days of relative obscurity, most teams had a banger or two. Unfortunately for us, the parish priest heard of our great win but he also heard of our 'banger'. He ordered that we return the

55

cup and medals. Such was the power and respect in which the parish priest was held that the club officials duly obliged, much to the disappointment of us all. My blind faith in the infallibility of the priest changed that day, as a questioning attitude penetrated my mind for the first time. It has never left me. I couldn't say much, though, as priests were everywhere in our family. I had two uncles priests in the diocese of Kerry, Fathers Brian and Laurence Kelly. I had two granduncles priests in England, Fathers Jerry and Pat Kelly, and I had two great granduncles priests. One great granduncle who had only been ordained for a few years got killed one dark night when he fell from his horse on his way to a sick call.

And just to show that sending back that cup and those precious medals didn't destroy the faith in the young Kellys, three of my brothers joined the religious life – two as priests and one as a Christian Brother. Unfortunately, Pádraig, who joined the De La Salle Order, died at thirty-nine years of age when he was Principal of St Fachtna's in Skibereen. My other two brothers are still ministering. Larry is now the parish priest and canon in Rathmore, Co. Kerry and Seamus is a missionary in Maracacbo in Venezuala since 1979. Ironically, he left Ireland for the mission fields the same day that Pope John Paul II left Ireland after his historic visit. They were on different planes!

My wife's family was also steeped in religion. Her late aunt, Sister Brenda, was a Presentation Sister who was totally deaf from the age of twenty-one as a result of meningitis and a cousin of hers, Father Dan Joe O'Sullivan, recently died in Chicago.

So, yes, we're practising Catholics. We brought up our family as Catholics but probably very differently from the way we were brought up ourselves. Certainly the rituals have changed. Television has put paid to many of those rituals. The 9 o'clock Rosary is now replaced by the 9 o'clock news and Benediction by some soap or other. Still the fundamentals are the same. In my first year as a teacher, I taught First Communion class in Kilmore West in Dublin 5. My wife Juliette taught First Communion for over twenty years in St Oliver's School in Killarney.

Funny the way religion evolves, or perhaps I should say the practice and manifestation of it. We are far more tolerant now. Respect has in many ways replaced ritual. A person's religion wouldn't make any difference to my attitude towards them, what religion they had if they had any religion at all. Indeed, I have had some great conversations with all sorts of people about religion or the lack of it in today's society. For me a truly religious person, a true follower of Christ and a true Catholic, respects everybody, be they papist, Presbyterian or Jew. Religion, like sport, should unite people, not divide them. This religious attitude of mine was central to my drive to open Croke Park to rugby and soccer. They were all sports people, they all deserved respect. If you could do your neighbour a good turn, like the good Samaritan, then you should do so. And that is the fundamental principle for me. Genuine respect leading to genuine generosity for the greater good.

I am no 'holy Mary' but I'd always be proud to say 'Yes, I am a Catholic, I am a proud member of the Catholic Church, despite whatever failings it may have.' And this brings me to a view point that has helped me sail steadfastly through many of the turmoils and scandals of recent decades. Some of God's messengers may err and have erred grievously, but that doesn't alter the message of God which denounces wrong-doing and evil and promotes all things good and fair. The fact that we are all equal in God's eyes is a great consolation as is the mantra, 'Judge not and you shall not be judged.' Yes, I always try to distinguish between the messenger and the message. A player can kick the ball wide from in front of the goals, but you don't blame the ball.

Still, I have a few small bees in my bonnet. Long sermons is one. If I were the Pope, I would bring in an edict confining all homilies to a maximum of five minutes. It might help get young people back to Mass. Maybe not just young people but older ones as well. I remember being at Mass a few years ago and a visiting priest started his homily by saying he'd be brief. He went on and on and when he finished, one old lady sitting beside me said to her friend, 'Good God, I thought he'd never stop. He spoke for twenty-nine minutes'. Another thing that I can never understand is why the Passion is read on Palm Sunday – the day our Lord entered Jerusalem in triumph. I know what happened during Holy Week but surely on Palm Sunday we should be concentrating on the triumph, the welcome before Our Lord had to hand back the medals (the palms) so to speak!

Having gone to school in St Brendan's College and having taught there for over thirty years, I saw first hand the great work done by so many priests over the years. But sadly, due to the decline in vocations, there are no priests there anymore. This has caused a lot of people to ponder where the Church is going. Recently Cardinal Seán Brady visited Killarney and he held an open forum one night. To the amazement of all, about five hundred people turned up – which shows that deep down many people care deeply about their Church and its future, whatever impression may be given elsewhere. I availed of the opportunity to ask him where he saw the Church being in tweny years' time in light of a rapidly ageing clergy and so few vocations. I asked would there be married priests, women priests, priests coming from abroad or would we see a return of vocations or would lay people take over. In reply, he stated that lay people will definitely have to be more active in running the Church. However, he didn't get into any observations on women priests or married priests. But my guess is that we will see one or the other or maybe both in the years ahead. Lay people won't do it all. They won't fill the gap that the priests, brothers and sisters have filled for generations. The sooner the Catholic Church addresses these key questions the sooner it will secure its future. And that is a mission that we have: to hand on the Catholic faith to future generations as it was handed down to us. That may mean a new type of priesthood doing what the religious have always done and providing leadership and direction to the faithful.

Another area the Church should move more decisively in is general as opposed to private confession. The key point is sorrow for one's sins. That is something between the individual and God. Is it necessary that a priest must hear a person's confession to be able to grant absolution? Not really, I would think. I have seen in the United States that general absolution is much more prevalent than here in Ireland. It's good that priests allow the laity to go to confession individually but I also feel that there should be more regular general confession. It is much easier on the individual and on the priest too, I should imagine. A general confession, if conducted with true humility and remorse, could be a powerful binding force within communities and create a sense of humility, but also responsibility, that individual confession may not be able to achieve. A public cleansing could be a mighty force for good and create a real sense of participation and binding in a congregation. The ceremony itself could be developed into a lovely religious experience. The point I want to stress here is that the congregation might be given a choice – have private confessions on one occasion and general absolution on another. I think this will happen more and more in the future and I welcome it.

To live is to change and change should lead to progress. The Catholic Church, somewhat like the GAA, has been slow to change. But that is not necessarily a bad thing. Still, I feel it should embrace certain changes a little quicker while at the same time sticking, as it has always done, to the core principles of our religion – respect and love of God and man. The application of that principle can vary with time. The message doesn't change but the messengers can and should be open to ways of getting the message across to a whole new world of the third millennium.

For me, I was born a Catholic, I like being a Catholic and I will stay a Catholic – warts and all – working at all times to eradicate the warts, but it is a challenging and slow process for the individual and for the Church. *Festina lente* but don't forget *Festina* entirely.

There is No Going Back

Mary O'Donnell

> Enough. Proclaim how good it is,
> perform your mighty offices,
> sit, stare, eternally, in state.
> Begin, it is already late.
> (Ágnes Nemes Nagy, *The Notebooks of Akhenaton*)

On 24 December 2008, I found myself in Monaghan Cathedral at Midnight Mass with my mother and daughter. The bishop's sermon was fluid and interesting. He had things to say, expressed with complexity and warmth. This Mass flowed theatrically, through its cycle of dramatic climax at the critical nexus of the consecration, on towards the plateau of communion. At this point I sensed the opening out to the great field of whatever it is we have in common as Catholics when we accept the bread and wine. I took Communion, came back to the pew and said a few prayers, which really amounted to rapid thoughts in the direction of this one and that one. I held the image of each person in my consciousness for perhaps only a few seconds, naming them, hoping for them. A friend with a broken heart after a love-affair, whose return to her home country has rekindled all the passion she thought she had banked down; a pair of bohemian, permanently broke friends; my husband in his beautiful atheism, that the clear light of his logic may long lean into him and add to his vision; my mother in old age, the fire of her personality glowing as she negotiates her life; my daughter in her mid-teens, as yet remarkably unscathed, clear-cut and idealistic. Long may she cling to idealism.

People close and not-so-close who have been near me in the past year rose to my consciousness. Opening things out, I decided to go on a world trip. The journey included Barack Obama and I prayed that he wouldn't be killed in the course of his work, and more importantly that he would be inspired to re-think the means of turning the Middle East Israeli-Palestinian war towards a political, constitutional resolution.

Anyone, in any religion, might do something similar. Praying for others is a common practice. But there I was, the vaulted roof of St Macartan's Cathedral above me, the choir singing like a well-schooled Protestant one, the organ lifting the congregation, and in my sights several people I knew or had once known when I was a girl. It was oddly comforting for someone who has developed an off-side relationship with Catholicism, who finds some of the dogma ridiculous, hypocritical and against the interests of the poor and of women.

* * *

I see myself as born a Christian and Catholic and still Catholic, though largely on my terms, which is another annoying thing for some people to hear. No thinking woman born in the 1950s who travelled the sometimes uncomfortable route from the 1960s to the 1990s could retain an allegiance to the old, McQuaid- and, in recent times, Connell-dominated Irish form of Catholicism. The obvious things affected women: the Church's undimmed interference in their biological lives, its obsession with human sexuality, its inability to accommodate the views of adults whose approach to life was not an exact match of the official template. Those were the obvious things to which I objected. But there was so much more, and my distrust of the 'old' Catholicism has only deepened with time.

Yet from time to time I am content enough to attend Mass. In some ways, the Church is like an errant partner who has failed and failed again, unfaithful to original promises of goodness, charity and honour, scurrilously cruel, distrustful, injurious and dishonest, not to say arrogant in the execution of an agreed brief. The only way, in the end, to accommodate a life with the partner is to accept the parts which still function and which have survived the malaise of its homocentric nature. And so, I accept the ritual of Mass because although Mass is communal it is also deeply private. It is this essential privacy in a very public place which fascinates me.

Catholicism and ritual are as interconnected as Islam and ritual, or Judaism and ritual. All have spent vast millions on architecture that expresses religious feeling, palatial sums for palatial buildings, whether we speak of the Vatican, or the Grand Mosque in (for example) Muscat, where it took three hundred women five years to weave the carpet on which several thousand men kneel and pray, guiltless expenditure while half the world is impoverished. There is not a religion on the planet which does not depend on ritual in some form of 'temple' for the execution of its high days of praise, sorrow, prayer and a kind of poetry. I use 'poetry' deliberately. Each religion derives some of its visual and auditory energies from the rhythms of seasons, nature, reproduction; each religion enhances its sense of itself by drawing on images from each of these and co-opting them into the ritual and verbal expression of belief.

Institutional Catholicism has always seemed to behave neurotically, as if it saw itself and its activities as moveable feasts. Then once a new move was incorporated and institutionalised, it went into immediate denial of that move, which was now sanctioned as part of 'tradition', as if it was divinely sanctioned whereas this is not, and never could be, the case. After all, priests once married, popes were married, and one pope I know of had children. There are many more examples of inconsistency. Inconsistency is one of the characteristics of human nature. But the sometimes frantic, sometimes complacent entity that is the Catholic Church is living through its own death-throes because it denies its own inconsistency and fails to run creatively with the notion of transformation and evolution generated by idea and need.

I remember giving a talk at a Catholic institution, during which I mentioned my hope that one day women would also be priests. The idea was greeted with a cynical snort from one member of the audience, who found it both comical and impossible. No spiritual grouping (and I include the Catholic Church within the term of reference 'spiritual grouping') that has shown a recognised antipathy towards females, that has prevented its own male priests who wish to be sexually active from being so, that opposes marriage and priesthood, that opposes women and priesthood, that has shown such knee-jerk responses to the long and sorry unravelling accounts of child abuse carried out by so many of its men, can seriously hope to earn my respect. Everything we ever suspect to have happened in relation to child abuse, but were unable to prove, has now been officially documented. The Church, as I see it, has a long way to go and there is no going back.

For some decades now, it has driven away the brightest and the best of its priests: the ones who didn't quite fit in – these included radical thinkers who cared as deeply about their own priesthood as they did about confronting the salient problems of the contemporary world for Catholics – and the ones who leaked the sexual repression of their situation, through carrying on long-term affairs with adult women (and men). Intellectual and homosexual priests suffered greatly during the 1970s in Ireland, most of them banished to some Father Ted-ish outpost that, it was hoped, would put manners on their antics. Those who would not be banished instead took up careers in distant Asian cities, in Europe, in South America – anywhere the orthodoxy could not catch them in its clutches, and where they found themselves needed. The interesting thing is that, even today, the natures of such men – diverse and tenacious as they are – have not been silenced. The spectacle of the gay Irish bishop exists among us. There are many gay Irish priests. And realistic people take it for granted that many priests, regardless of orientation, are not celibate at all.

* * *

On another level, the sharing in a religious imagination (mine, connected with a praying collective) is importantly connected to my sense of myself as a writer/artist. Because religion and art share things: they teach the practitioner to attend to the small details of life that are the pivot-points on which the spirit thrives; they insist on habitual practice if either is to develop a deepening relationship between self and the world or the cosmos; and they demand – if they are to develop – the right to be unorthodox. In other words, in thinking as a writer and a person with some religious feeling, there is always another horizon to be crossed. I am reminded of Botticelli who, in painting his *Primavera*, takes the story of the Virgin and marries history and myth in a lyrical composition that expresses the joy of spring, growth and new beginnings. This is what the human imagination is best suited to engaging with – semi-religious ideas, the mythical, the archetypal. It is instinctively programmed to interpret and re-interpret as it thinks fit, as each person's life evolves, not disconnected but very connected to the cosmic creative force that is the precursor to all formal religious expressions.

Yet historically, artistic expression and cultural values have more often than not been compromised, often by political or religious systems or both, and the struggle between what appeals to our base natures and our higher natures is nothing unusual. Visionaries abound, yet the world today is flooded with artistic malpractice, especially in performance art – from dancing bears and Coke-drinking camels, to Amsterdam family porn shows and pole-dancing in Allenwood, to a range of more subtle performance that appeals also to our base natures. Because, as Mr Gradgrind said in *Hard Times*, 'People must be entertained.'

But what entertains us and nourishes us? And why is sexuality and what we do with it so often the nub of so much debate in both religions and artistic arenas if it is not, essentially, the essential root of our human natures?

As I have already pointed out, the Orthodox Churches are also littered with examples of unsteady practice that reflects the flawed humanity of the institution. Back in the 1970s and 1980s, everything that one ever suspected might be occurring within the rank and file of the institutionalised Catholic Church, but could not then prove, came to be public knowledge and the sorry unravelling of the garment of deception is not yet over.

The fact is, religion and art are diminishable and sometimes diminished. But both are as strong or as feeble as those who invest their lives in the practice of either. They have the capacity to strengthen by challenging us to investigate the manner in which we live, and the purpose of our ordinary heroism.

Most Irish people's first experience of art came through being in a church, finding themselves seated and silent for an hour once a week. I remember scanning the high ceilings of the church, or perhaps out of boredom sometimes allowed my eyes to follow the images of the Stations, or study the statues, or the elaborate glint of stitching on a priest's robes. The chalice and other altar vessels were visually arresting. These were special vessels designed for a singular and unusual feast. Everywhere, through our experience of church, while the ordinary Sunday morning odours of families rose around us – the breakfast smells, the hint of farmyard work, the perfumed women with mantillas – came visual paragraphs from a mysterious story. There was a woman with a snake beneath her plaster feet; and a carpenter who could have been anybody's father out about the yard, doing the jobs; and there might have been a St Theresa, and lilies. Church was a space in which a crown of blue lit stars surrounded a Virgin's head. It was a space in which the agony of a man whose body had fallen to suffocation and death through hanging on the cross, might be imagined.

All this might be accompanied by music – a dubious choir and sometimes good choirs for the day of high sacrifice – Good Friday – and then the morning of dancing sun, Easter Sunday – when once again images of eggs, oestrus and the completion of the life cycle were borne into our consciousness.

So through the experience of church, as a child, I first discovered the following: architecture as *art* – for all churches are designed to make those who inhabit them feel a sense of wonder. They are supposed to make us aspire, feel better, look up and beyond our physical selves, to try to connect with an unstated greatness beyond our immediate concerns. I discovered also religious art and music; and stories.

Art was about raising oneself in the direction of the beautiful and the good. I believe I would not be the writer I am today had I not experienced Catholicism. That doesn't mean I would not be a writer, but I would be a very different one, not lesser, not greater, but different.

As a Catholic who responds to her religion in terms of ethics rather than dogma – on a philosophical level (as opposed to a day-to-day utilitarian one), I still see no essential conflict between the idea of religion and the idea of culture in today's Ireland, despite the fact that traditionally they have been diametrically opposed. What I do recognise in both is a sense of justified shame that both stand accused of elitism, of exclusionism, of not always drawing on the difficult, imprisoned or restricted aspects of our society.

Like art, religion announces a better way. Yet most cultural practitioners by and large do not presume to 'know best' except within the range of their work. Some religious practitioners, in contrast, by virtue of the fact that they are the official envisioners of the infinite and divine, have traditionally presumed very much to know what is good for all. Yet I can't seriously object to this position by saying 'everything is relative', when I do not believe that. Relativism is jaded and open to exploitation. Things are not always necessarily relative, although they can be. Ironically, along with ideals such as truth, justice, beauty and revelation, much of that shared by religion and culture has to do with the word *love*. Christians are urged to 'Love one another', to turn from violence, to recognise that one's negative reaction is one's own problem; artists explore love, and its variant moods – violence, hatred, war, creation, destruction; they explore the self at odds with social and political culture; the act of creating something out of nothing is also, oddly, an act of love, because above all activities it integrates the human personality and connects it to something beyond the ego-bound self.

The question for Catholicism today may be how to interrogate essential subjects ceatively, such as Self and society; Self and how to be *good*; Self and the inevitability of death. The painter Brian Maguire has done huge canvasses depicting the lives of prisoners, of torture-victims; Brian Bourke works on the level of Irish myth and archetype; the novelists of our day – John Banville, Colm Tóibín, Jennifer Johnston – show characters struggling for one fleck of self-forgiveness in a largely unforgiving world. My own work concerns itself, in its fictional expression, with people who lead conventional lives but are in fact struggling, sometimes violently, for liberation from the casement of social civility. The local is circumscribed often positively by the global, yet the local struggles for autonomy that is neither repressive nor anachronistic.

In my poetry, which is the closest I come to true religious expression, I explore landscape, the senses, the history of women's lives, love, sexuality, childbirth, the challenge of family history. My deepest religious feeling arises through poetry, because only then do I feel reconnected to the cosmos. In beauty and the perception of beauty, I can feel myself re-attuned to the idea of the godly. For me at such times, there are no barriers between the religious and the artistic. I'm idealistic enough to believe that I can occasionally touch the tree of paradise where religious feeling and art are at one.

* * *

Yet I am still a Catholic. I have absorbed the childhood sentences and explanations – some of them profoundly illogical – about body and blood, I have discarded them for years, finding them useless and insensible. Yet belief in the infinite, in mystery, in the invisible, does not – contrary to what some commentators believe – present a soft core, a prettified approach to the divine. On the contrary, it makes demands on the individual to remember that the animal self is not only adequate to all this mystery, but in fact may be the key. There is no division between animal self and spiritual self when human nature is integrated, and the latter is not in some manner 'superior' to the former. The challenge, again, is to live in the beauty of the flesh, and know that it is adequate, that it is glorious, that it is as it is intended to be.

Catholicism poured more sensuousness into my already sensuous younger nature, hunting me down like young prey to be reformed, through the round of confession and self-scrutiny, I believe. The development of an active conscience was one of its gifts, but a distorted one, that led to over-scrupulosity in some, and to great guilt-laden pain in others. The fact that my own family was not sternly over-religious was ultimately liberating for me, because that allowed me to make choices. And although Catholicism partially seduced with its images and scents – the kind of thing that enrages committed atheists – with its contrasts of pleasure and pain, in adult life I came to see the hunter in a different light. I am aware, but I also remind myself to beware of distortions of language, of false religious idiom, of men who believe they can speak for women. It threatens some and creates either neurotic mystics or mystic neurotics. The 'saints' who were ecstatics were flesh-and-blood people who followed a trail of severe contrasts to the farthest possible horizon. Hence John of the Cross, Teresa of Avila, Ignatius Loyola and others. The fortunate among them slipped away without formulating a dogma for the rest of the world to follow. As for the rest? We live and wait.

A Communion of Sinners?

Enda McDonagh

> We shall not cease from exploration
> And the end of all our exploring
> Will be to arrive where we started
> And know the place for the first time.
> (T. S. Eliot, *Little Gidding*)

If you come from a tiny bog village in East Mayo you are, with ninety percent of your school-mates and peers, almost compelled to leave it and to explore the larger and more exciting(?) world beyond. And if you are born into the Catholic Church, its apparently endless inner exploration can sometimes lead one to the beyond of religions and rituals, beliefs and unbeliefs, never dreamt of in the cradle country of your baptism. As student, priest and academic who has had the opportunity to work, wonder and wander around the world without completely cutting the umbilical chord with village and Church of birth and baptism, I have more than once arrived back where I started and got once again to know the place for the first time. So what being a Catholic means to me has a history of exploration and return, adventure and frustration, which forms a much longer story than I can attempt to tell here.

What I can attempt to tell, or better to illustrate, is something of the prevailing winds and of the choppy, at times raging, waters which accompanied these voyages around my Father (God) and of the guiding stars and human navigators who got me from time to time safely into the home port, and of what I found and find there.

It is unfortunate, perhaps on reflection providential, that I begin this essay on 21 May 2009 bombarded by media accounts of and comments on the *Report of the Commission to Inquire into Child Abuse* presided over by Judge Sean Ryan which was issued yesterday. I say providential because long overdue, full public rehearsal of their pain for the abused persons and of the utterly shameful behaviour by some members of the Catholic Church and its leaders was still essential. It shatters once again the complacency into which believers, clerical and lay, too readily fall when the latest scandal has disappeared from the news headlines. For if my voyages in Catholicism have taught me anything over my sixty years of adulthood, it is that we are first and foremost a communion of sinners who in our best moments aspire to be a communion of saints. Of course there are real and persistent saints among us, mainly invisible and unknown, but we would be well advised, especially if bishops, clergy or religious, to recognise our primarily sinful status and the humility, indeed humiliation, that should go with it. How this also allows us to speak of the Church as the Body or Bride of Christ or to share what we call Holy Communion will re-appear later.

Recognising the sinfulness within and without us, in person and community, is part of the gift of being Catholic. Jesus reserved his harshest words for the self-righteous, the blind leading the blind, the hard of heart, those seeking the first places in synagogue and at table. Some of his unlikely heroes, then as now, were the socially and religiously excluded, the publican at the back of the temple, the Roman soldier who deemed himself unworthy to receive Jesus into his house, the Good Samaritan, and Christ's own criminal companion on the near-by cross. The list goes on and on. And it is home to that forgiven and forgiving company that every generation of Catholics must find its way and know the place perhaps for the first time. That is what makes the occasion of this reflection on being a Catholic in the midst of the Church in public disgrace truly providential.

Prodigal sons and daughters, as we all always to some extent are, and not necessarily acceptable to the righteous elder brothers and sisters who await us, we are driven by a deeper sense of shame and suffering and then by a hope of welcome and forgiveness that will transform us anew. The prodigally loving Father knows how to celebrate our return, our many returns, as we continue to stray in search of power, privilege, self-righteousness or simply pleasure. We may not be up to seven times a day, but the falls and stumbles persist

The providential emergence into the light of recent and current serious falls is, of course, the first coming of the Light, of the Light of the world in Johannine terms and so more crucially Light for the Church. The crux is, as the Gospel notes, whether we are willing to acknowledge the Light and act on it. By mid-June we may not be really able to boast of 'green shoots', as those other troubled institutional leaders in banking, finance and politics assert, yet our own glimmers of light may be perceived. The debates in the media, the more positive responses of religious and political leaders and above all the strong public reaction to the March of the Abused on Wednesday 10 June, could lead to serious repentance and restitution. But the many words of apology are no substitution for acts of restitution. And how far will such restitution be left to groups and individuals directly responsible, who were also often themselves exploited, oppressed or at best ignored in their limitations as well as in their failures due to internal Church structural injustice?

Yet the light is emerging for those with eyes to see although it may still reveal just more of our own shabbiness. The shabbiness can and will be shed, but not without our co-operation and not by our own power. The immediate bearers of the light are undoubtedly the abused. Keeping our eyes and attention fixed on them will draw us more deeply into the forgiving, liberating and transforming light of the God of Jesus Christ, by whose power everything, as Bernanos noted, becomes grace. It may be a slow transformation for all of us. Our inevitable if diminishing resistance and righteous anger by the abused will not disappear overnight or overyear. Yet the grandeur and grace of God will not be finally stayed: 'Because the Holy Ghost over the bent/ World broods with warm breast and with ah! Bright wings.' Hopkins' concluding words to his poem 'God's Grandeur' re-

main the key to the recovery from the present crisis of the
Church in Ireland and elsewhere. It is that Holy Spirit that I trust
in to enable me to be a genuine if fragile Catholic today. Of
course, there is more, much more to be said. Only some of it can
be briefly rehearsed here.

Praise as prayer and self-healing are primary tasks for the
mutilated Church. Out of that self-reform inspired by the Spirit
and the Church-reform demanded by the secular world and no
less the work of the Spirit, the Church in turn attends to the
mutilated world, God's world. The Jewish psalms, the long tradition of Christian prayer originating in the prayer which Jesus
taught us, provide the models for our praise and its call for
ecclesial, social and cosmic healing. 'Hallowed be thy name: thy
kingdom come' summarise these dimensions of praise and healing. Only in the final coming of the kingdom, which the Church
is called to serve, will the praise and healing be complete. As the
praise issues into service, the charter of service itself is sum-
marised in the Beatitudes with their further elaboration in the
Sermon on the Mount and the extended gospels. Some of these
are particularly apt to the broken structures of the Church and of
the human community as a whole, and indeed to planet earth in
its brokenness and despoliation.

The justice seekers and the peace-makers of the Beatitudes
outline basic vocations for all Church members. These vocations
of justice and peace include the whole range of human relationships and communities and their planetary inheritance. At present the justice and peace-making apply very urgently to the
mutilated and divided Catholic Church and to the wider and af-
flicted Christian community. What it means to be a Catholic
today, in a practising sense, is to be able to translate the praise
and prayer into the promotion of justice within the Church itself
as demanded and as long prelude to the achieving of ecclesial
reconciliation and peace. The perfunctory greeting of peace at
Mass or the declining and often casual sacramental practice of
reconciliation, are no substitutes for the surrender to justice and
restitution by individual Catholics, by ecclesial power-figures

and their protective structures. To be a Catholic is to begin, at serious personal and status cost, on the long road to justice and so to peace.

There are renewal centres on the way. The Eucharist so central to Catholic Christianity has the potential to provide food and shelter, healing companionship to the pilgrims for justice and peace and encourage them on their way. If it is not trivialised in indifferent celebration on the one hand or ideologised in some worn-out form on the other, the Eucharist remains at the heart of Catholic life and transformation. To be a Catholic is to enter a community of repentance and humility and so follow the itinerary of Christ's and of the Church's life, death and resurrection. The Body of the Lord as community has broader and more profound implications still.

As indicated earlier, *Catholic* in origin means *universal*. In recent times and particularly after Vatican II, but not only then, the universal or rather the universe of salvation has tended to follow the range of the reign of God announced by Jesus and indeed that of creation. It was after all in and through the Word of God, Jesus the Christ (John, Paul) that all things were created and it was into the world so loved by God that he sent his Son as Saviour. There are many unresolved issues still to be sorted out theologically in the affirmation of the availability of salvation to all within and without the Catholic/Christian community. For this Catholic the basic affirmation is the undeniable reality of the love of God and of God as love. In such a vision all human beings are subject to and transformed by the reign of God. We are all daughters and sons of the one God, even if that is explicitly recognised by only a few. Whereas as members of one another in Christian terms where if one suffers we all suffer, in secular terms it is frequently and equivalently asserted that if the human rights of one are violated then the human rights of all are violated. These Christian and secular claims are as equivalent in principle and as they are frequently neglected in practice.

A number of former and perhaps current Irish Catholics have been known to say that they do not believe in an afterlife.

Without quibbling about the appropriateness of the word 'afterlife', I would prefer to reflect on how our earthly bonding as believers or unbelievers may continue beyond the worldly separation of death. Of course the resurrection of Jesus (no simple 'afterlife') is the immediate source of our Christian and Catholic belief. Various rationalist attempts to undermine the evidence for it strike me, after years of reflection and occasional hesitations, as invalid. There are older if less powerful supporting arguments and convictions confirming that death is not the end of all. Perhaps for many even committed Catholics the simple absence of the other and the sheer lack of communication is the hardest to bear and the easiest route to loss of faith in the continued existence of the deceased. However, the Catholic understanding of membership of Christ's Body, in principle available to all, enables one to see the departed loved one as still living in Christ and still living if inarticulately in us. The sweep of the reign of God includes naturally those who have gone before us as it will include those who come after us. For that reign establishes a democracy of the living and the dead, whose earthly lives entitled them to that participation. Our memories, their genetic legacies, family and social traditions, and in some cases at least their saintly example, artistic and political achievements enable our ancestors to continue to influence the development of that great democracy of God's reign or kingdom towards final fulfilment in equality, justice and the peace (shalom) that is flourishing of all creatures together with their God.

That final return to the earth from which we came will indeed be the end of all our exploring and ensure knowing the place for the first and most glorious time in the company of its Creator God and all our fellow-travellers.

A Radical Faith

Finola Bruton

I was born in Westport in September 1952. Like, I presume, most other families in the country we said the Rosary every night and our mother always said night prayers with us as we lay in the bed ready for sleep or devilment as the case may have been. We went to Mass every Sunday where the entrance was guarded carefully by a tall man whose job it was to collect thruppence from every individual regardless of station or income.

The summer months were spent on Island More in Clew Bay and the Rosary, with all the trimmings, was even longer there than at home. On Sundays, weather permitting, we set out on the long journey to Mass by boat and then by foot. It must have taken us two or three hours to get there. Dick always preferred to row rather than use the engine which made the journey even longer. Dressed in our wellies and jumpers we bailed out the water with old paint cans and settled into a wonderful commune with nature, running our fingers through the cool green sea, watching the fish and listening to the gulls until we arrived at the shore of the mainland. There we deposited our wellies and watched Nellie don her good hat and good shoes for the two or three mile walk to Carrowholly Church.

We were never allowed to look around at the few cars coming from behind which might, of course, have indicated that we were looking for a lift. But we were rewarded after Mass with a bag of sweets before we began the journey back to the island. Such was the seriousness with which the Catholic religion was taken in those dark economic times. It was a commitment with which I was wholly happy. It always left me with a sense of togetherness and a contentment that God was with us and looking after us. There was no question but that he was there and that we had an obligation to honour and glory and revere him. I have never had an issue with that, then or since.

We were taught by the Mercy Sisters and the Christian Brothers respectively. We always started our classes with a prayer, said the Angelus at noon and were immersed in the study and retention of the old catechism throughout our primary school days. We were, of course, leading up to and preparing for Confirmation at the age of twelve. We had to know that catechism inside out as we were all going to be asked one question by the bishop. There was no way we could let ourselves or our teacher down by flunking on that question. There was always an aura of mystery about the convent and the lives of the sisters who lived there. There were rumours that they liked boxes of chocolates and they always walked out in pairs. This was something in my teenage years with which I could not agree and only much later could understand the source from which such rules were based.

I have never had any difficulty with the sisters and, with one or two exceptions, loved and enjoyed them. The episodic acts of cruelty by one individual or the harsh corporal punishments meted out by her or some of the Christian Brothers were difficult to witness or to understand. But they always seemed to me to belong to those people themselves and to be separate from God who was watching from above and would always mind us. Besides, such acts of cruelty were even more prevalent in families throughout the land as recent evidence demonstrates. This is not to condone them or protect any individual or community but simply to place them in the context of the lives of many people struggling to survive in difficult times. The film *Ryan's Daughter* is a good indicator of the harshness existing in those times in Irish society. Synge and, later, John McGahern were to write memorably of such painful episodes either in their own lives or in those of society at large.

I thank God every day for that first eighteen years of my life and for the gift of faith. To have known God from the very beginning is a privilege and a blessing. To have learned to pray from an early age is a gift incomparable with any other, save life itself. To have been baptised a Catholic is to owe a debt of gratitude to God the Father, God the Son and God the Holy Spirit. The fact of these blessings is, at least in my mind, superior to and apart from the imperfect manner in which they often have been and will continue to be carried out. Each and every organisation, religious or otherwise, has by its very nature its own power struggles, its own battle between good and evil. Institutions are human. This simple fact, however, does not, and ought not, prevent us from using our critical faculties. Criticism does not diminish our faith, nor should it diminish our love of God or of the Church.

I first learned the art of reflective criticism from the late Dominican Priest, Father Fergal O'Connor. He was a breath of fresh air to UCD students in the 1960s and 1970s. His scholarly mind and compassionate soul gave a new dimension to what being a Catholic was really all about. Never having questioned anything in our youth, he showed us just how to do that but always with a watchful eye on those human prejudices that might have us believe that we could bring the whole edifice tumbling down without any consequences, that we could have rights without obligations, power without responsibilities, that we could take positions without a continuous examination of our own motives. He taught us that the role of self critique was pivotal and the tendency towards self deception enormous. He set up Ally, the organisation for unmarried mothers in the 1960s. Concern in society about the unmarried mother was not only about the moral wellbeing or otherwise of these girls, but was influenced greatly by the property considerations and implications that might follow. The prospect of conferring legitimacy on these children struck fear in the hearts of families throughout the land. It was the fear for property and the fear for money. This fear drew strength from the moral attitudes of the Catholic hierarchy. It seemed at times as if the two came together to be complicit in the culture of shame and disapprobation that was widespread in the country.

For all that, it must never be forgotten that when parents throughout the country were banishing their pregnant daughters from their homes, and leaving children as orphans, the Church was providing the only places of sanctuary for them. Were it not for the Church, some of the alternatives open to these girls might have been much worse. It was, of course, entirely understandable that the Church would reflect the society it served. It would not have retained the loyalty of its flock had it not done so. But it was not passive either. It was not only in the care for unmarried mothers that the Church gave a lead in practical compassion well ahead of that displayed either in the United Kingdom or later by the native government. Where would Ireland have been without the hospitals and schools built and staffed by the Church? A whole network of voluntary organisations created by the Church enabled Irish people to enjoy advanced social services, without having to submit to the dead hand of government bureaucracy.

The decline in the power and authority of the Catholic Church was well advanced by the time the sexual abuse scandals hit the headlines. Liberalism and feminism had become established forces in Irish society. They had their own agendas. The love of one's Church, at least the Catholic Church, was not one of them. The expression of that love was poorly received and at times outrightly derided. By the late 1980s and early 1990s the battle to be and remain a committed Catholic had begun. I had never before felt the need to fight for my religious beliefs. They were there, assumed, given and rock solid. How could anyone, let alone so many, turn so suddenly from the source of life, of goodness and of all eternity? Lapses from Church services, the breaking of Church rules, and the human sins of us all were understandable. But the hardness of heart of so many that was now emerging was as disturbing as it was surprising.

The cultural context had indeed changed. Dinner party conversation had changed. Media dialogue had changed. Family conversations had changed. It was as if everybody was outside looking in, poking fun at the Church, at the priests and at the whole idea of the sacraments. The language of Christianity was *passé*. God was being driven into the private sphere, where it was thought but not said that he might do less damage to the new thinking in an emerging affluent and restraint-free society. I remember one dinner party conversation where a leading feminist was patiently explaining to me that it was, you know, normal for a woman to have feelings and desires to procreate. And that one would keep having them. The clear implication being that, really, one had to rise above these feelings and take control of your life and your femininity and prioritise career. These feminists were reacting to the Church telling them how to behave but were unable to see that *they* were now telling me how to behave. My behaviour was now to be modelled on their credos and not on those of my God and my hope.

To speak Catholic, to do Catholic and to be Catholic was to risk being cold-shouldered, ridiculed and silenced, often through an array of social mannerisms and etiquette that would have seemed impolite to breach. You were regarded as old fashioned, stuck in a time warp, belonging to another era, were you to breach these social protocols, either in private or in public. Even to refer to one's religious conviction was to risk giving 'offence' to someone. This was modern tolerance.

The media, during this period, was unashamedly skewed in its coverage of social and political and religious events. It was secular, liberal and critical of most things Catholic. On one occasion I addressed a public meeting organised by Women in the Home. One of the most enlightening speeches that I ever heard was given at this seminar by an American Professor. When I enquired about his making media appearances, I was told that every radio and television show had turned him down. Some time later a march by the feminists for better crèche facilities was flagged for weeks by a leading newspaper. Huge numbers were due to turn up. On the appointed day in question a hundred people were given great coverage in the same newspaper. Meanwhile down in Galway thirty thousand people were attending a Novena. They got no coverage at all. Early morning radio reports were in later years forced to take due note, if only because of resultant traffic congestion.

Being a Catholic in the 1990s and the early years of the new millennium was for me a painful experience. Little sustenance was to be found amongst my peer group. Overall the Church seemed to be paralysed. Priests had retreated in the face of explosive abuse scandals. Some crumbs of comfort could be found in the religious articles and magazines. It was in these sources that the best intellectual rigor, depth and universal truths were to be found, in contrast to the opinion makers in the media who, by and large, were either stale, ignorant or on a rant, exorcising their latest angst. They made no difference to people's moral or spiritual growth. They gave no meaning to people's lives.

These observations led me to start my own rearguard reaction. I endeavoured to go to daily Mass. I attended Eucharistic adoration. I became a minister of the Eucharist. I began to revisit Knock. I prayed the Rosary as always. I wrote for the *St Martin Magazine*. I joined the Board of *The Irish Catholic* newspaper. I wish that I could say that I became morally transformed. I didn't. But I learned and am learning how much I need God in my life.

Being Catholic is and has always been about that hunger for God. Catholicism through its magnificent sacraments, through the Mass, through prayer and through other like-minded individuals, has fed that need. The concept of grace has been pivotal.

The last five years in the United States have taught me more about what being a Catholic is all about than the previous fifty in Ireland. Here I have had the opportunity to watch EWTN, a cable television channel devoted to all things Catholic. In high quality programmes the teachings of the Church are explored in an adult and intellectually satisfying way. It struck me that this is what has been missing for many years. While the public is now more educated both in general and in so many specialist fields than ever before, education of Catholics in religious issues has not kept pace. Even though Pope Benedict XVI has argued convincingly for the compatibility of faith and reason, many adult Catholics are starved of opportunities to explore their religious beliefs to intellectual depths consistent with the depth with which much less important issues are explored.

Listening, on EWTN, to so many converts explain their journey towards the Catholic Church, on the programme *The Journey Home*, the beauty, the significance and the richness of Catholicism shines through. The Church that Christ founded becomes real, peopled by believers in that great miracle of two thousand years ago. Those who, as adults, have chosen to join the Catholic faith can see this richness and uniqueness more clearly than those of us who have been born into it. The education in Catholic faith that one receives in preparation for First Holy Communion and Confirmation and in religious education classes in schools is not sufficiently durable to sustain Catholics through adult life in modern times. Just as people need constant renewal and training for employment in changing economic and technological conditions, all Catholic adults need a similar process to help in applying their faith in the changing conditions of their own lives and in the world around them. The Church needs to find a way of making such opportunities available in forms that are suitable to the busy, stress-filled lives of modern Catholics. It needs to look at its resources among the priests and laity to ensure that it deploys them in a way that fulfils this vital educational mission in the modern world.

In many ways, what is needed is a lay revolution. One that asks us to evangelise – 'a new evangelisation', as Pope John Paul II asked of us. A revolution that starts in the home and in the community. A revolution where we challenge the secularist notion that evangelisation is somehow 'offensive' or disturbing of the public peace. All change requires some measure of disturbance and Catholics need to be free to put forward the radical message of Christ in a way that is both sympathetic and challenging to prevailing notions. Within the Church one must challenge the notion that one can be a cultural Catholic, using the rituals as a support without believing in their full significance. We need to question the idea that we do not require to commit ourselves to the Church, to its rituals and ceremonies and rules, to its request that we behave ourselves as decent human beings. And to question the idea that as we may be saved anyway, that being part of a Church is not a path to salvation. This is just what Christ asks of us. To be part of his Church. To follow in his footsteps. This is what being Catholic is all about. Catholicism for me is a radical faith. It was its radical nature that crucified Jesus. Its radicalism lies in the fact that it challenges our very being, our thought processes. It asks us to look into our hearts and question our desires and motivations. It refuses to let us escape from the reality of our condition, from our propensity to pretend that we are what we are not. From our yearning to be seen as we wish to be seen and not, as the humility of the saints teaches us, as we really are: weak, dependent and utterly at the mercy of God.

The Catholic faith sets out how we must think about each other and how we must live with one another. Its rules and regulations are based on a profound understanding of human nature. These rules are a support, a crutch, if you like, to keep us from the worst excesses in ourselves. The Church demands that we seek the truth in ourselves so that we can spare others the injustices that automatically follow our constant subterfuge and deceit. The deception of one can be the destruction of another. This is to ask people to emerge from the cave, as Plato might have it, and face the light and truth of human reality. It is by its very nature, a painful process and one that can put us at odds with ourselves and with the God of our creation. It is little wonder then, that in every age there have been many who might wish to stop this radical religion. Challenging us as it does, it can be a lonely and very difficult path. And yet it is the great hope of our lives, Christ, through the Church, forgiving us as we fall again and again. The Church that is our refuge and our companion. The Church that needs us, the laity, to dedicate ourselves towards its wellbeing and towards the wellbeing of its guardians.

A Cradle Catholic

Conor Brady

For more than forty years I have been a writer, a journalist, an editor. But I have never before sat down at my screen (or, in pre-electronic days, at my typewriter) to answer the question: What does it mean to me to be Catholic? I ask myself why I never did so. Part of the answer, I know, is that I dislike reductionism and stereotyping. I resist putting people into categories or boxes. The human being is too complex for that.

I was raised in a Catholic Church that excelled in the categorising and excluding of people. It cut off whole categories of supposed sinners from the comfort of the sacraments. It excluded its members from attending certain schools and colleges. It categorised the souls of dead babies on the basis that some went to limbo and some to heaven. It marked out the road to salvation in terms that seemed to exclude most of the human race.

It defined a 'zone of salvation' that for many of us appeared to be virtually unattainable. Any breach of the vast, complex set of rules and regulations was to have oneself cast outside of that zone, bound for eternal damnation.

This was the 1950s. Memories of the Eucharistic Congress of 1932, the great public pageant, staged to proclaim the triumph of the Catholic Church in an Irish State, were still fresh. The hierarchy and the clergy ran virtually everything, from the schools of philosophy in the universities to the hospitals to the parish schools.

My sister decided that she wanted to marry what was then referred to as a 'non-Catholic'. The clergy at her home parish determined there could be no ceremony in 'their' church. So she and her husband-to-be went to London where a relative serving as a curate in the Diocese of Westminster obliged.

My sister had a wonderful, happy marriage for almost forty years until she lost her husband to cancer. They had three children and, in time, seven grandchildren, all of whom have enriched our lives. But this was all against the Church's rules, of course, and should never have happened.

So I dislike any process that seeks to isolate me or cut me off from the greater part of humanity that is not Catholic. The Catholicism in which I was reared sought to do that and, I believe, did so very consciously.

Outside the Catholic Church, we were told, there is no salvation (*Extra esslesia nulla salus*). There were sub-clauses to this rule. A Protestant might be saved if he had an aspiration to belong to the True Faith – if he were simply misguided in his Protestantism. A savage in the jungle could be saved if he had a yearning to know and love God but hadn't actually met Catholic missionaries. Generally, however, only Catholics – real or aspirant – could hope for heaven.

It wasn't just the Catholic Church that operated these fiercely exclusionary rules. I grew up in a midland town with a mix of faiths that dated back to the Plantations. There were churches for the Anglicans, the Methodists and the Presbyterians. There was a Quaker meeting house and even a Free Masons' lodge.

The Protestants were just as insistent as the Catholics that they should have no unnecessary truck with outsiders. Mostly they ran businesses or were farmers. They did not want to dilute their communities. So they had their own schools, their own clubs and they married their own. Later, when we met in adult life, some of the Protestant children that I had known told me that they had been conditioned to regard us as idolaters.

I was probably just saved from a lifetime of such isolationism by Vatican II. I was thirteen in 1962 when the Council opened and I was coming up to my Leaving Certificate year when it closed in 1965.

The ecumenical tide that flowed from the Council did not reach all shores at the same time or with the same strength. But it reached the Cistercians at Roscrea where I was a boarder, providing a vigorous agenda for debating societies and for discussions in religion class.

It extended through the years in which I took my primary degree at UCD. Religion and faith featured in the mix of ideas that we argued over in Earlsfort Terrace – even if the debates about contending political ideologies drew larger crowds.

After graduation, when I started as a trainee journalist at *The Irish Times*, I found myself working in an environment in which most of my colleagues and all of the key, senior people were Protestants. I came to know many of them well, to trust them and to rely upon them. Some became good friends over the years.

Increasingly, I found myself coming to realise that little of real significance separated me from them or made them different. They had traditions to which I was a stranger. They had things like the Boys' Brigade and the Mothers' Union that Catholics did not join. They had Harvest Thanksgiving and Evensong. They had their own special charities and hospitals that they supported. Some of them even had fathers who were ministers of religion.

But by and large they had the same values, the same life principles and were susceptible to the same weaknesses as anyone else. If anything, they had a more developed understanding of the ideal of 'good works' than was common among Catholics of my acquaintance.

Once, when I used the term 'Catholic' in some working context, a Church of Ireland colleague said: 'Don't you mean Roman Catholic?' He considered his Church to be Catholic – but not Roman; that is to say, under the authority of the Pope.

So was there – is there – any difference between me and my Protestant colleagues of those days? Does being a Catholic make me a better person, a more moral person, a person more pleasing in the sight of God? Does it give me a spiritual benefit or benefits that I would not otherwise have?

I cannot possibly claim any moral 'edge' over those people. I cannot say that I live a life that is any more in conformity with the tenets of Christianity than theirs. I cannot say that the teaching of Jesus has shaped my values any more than it has done for them.

In truth, I am not a very conforming Catholic. I disagree with the Church's teaching on many issues. *Humanae Vitae* was and is, in my view, an incoherent document. I disagree profoundly with the Vatican stance on clerical celibacy and on women priests. I am a sporadic rather than a regular attendee at the sacraments. I believe in the Real Presence at the celebration of the Eucharist. But I cannot accept that my God is contained within molecules of flat dough and fermented grape juice.

My lifelong experience as a journalist and in particular my tenure as Editor of *The Irish Times* for 16 years yielded few positive encounters with the men who ran the Irish Catholic Church at the very highest levels. And while one might attempt to differentiate between the individual and the institution, it is impossible not to measure the 'anima' or spirit of an organisation, at least in part, by the people who direct it.

There were none who allowed themselves to be heard speaking with the frankness of Archbishop Diarmaid Martin or with the humanity of Bishop Willie Walsh. I suspect that at this point some readers may say, 'This person is not a Catholic at all.' All I can plead in response is that, notwithstanding, I still cannot regard myself as being anything other than Catholic.

So what does my Catholicism, flawed, imperfect and questioning as it is, give to me? Does it provide me with me anything beyond a label, a badge of identity, an aesthetically pleasing liturgy and a tradition that can be traced back two thousand years or so?

I ask myself: Do I consider myself a Catholic simply because this has always been, by accident of birth, my point of spiritual reference? The term 'cradle Catholic' comes to mind.

Do I need Catholicism as distinct from any other Christian faith to realise God's goodness, to know that God loves me personally and individually and to understand that when my temporal life ends I will be united again with my Creator?

And what do I bring to Catholicism? What do I give back to

the community of faith in which I was raised and within whose embrace I seek to live my life, however imperfectly and inadequately?

In truth, I bring to my faith but a poor offering of myself. I am a sinner and a doubter. Yet I comfort myself with the knowledge that so too were at least some of Christ's apostles. I suppose, if nothing else, I help to make up the numbers.

But in spite of the doubting sentiments set out above and based on my life experience, I like Catholicism. Perhaps I even love it – in the same way that one can love a family member whose flaws and shortcomings will raise the blood-pressure of everyone around them.

I love the immense variety of spiritual richness that Catholicism offers. There is an almost limitless range of choice in deciding where to fix one's spiritual focus. For some it is the *persona* of Jesus. For others it may be upon Mary the Blessed Mother. Men of my father's generation – identifying perhaps with the role of provider – were devoted to St Joseph. Many Catholics have favourite saints or angels. I know one woman who prays only to and through St Michael the Archangel. I know another who is devoted exclusively to St Pio of Pietrelcina – better known as Padre Pio.

In my own case, I generally find my spiritual focus – however inadequate it may be – through the contemplative Cistercian/Benedictine tradition. I owe that to my education in Roscrea.

I have but a very poor and limited insight into the spiritual dynamics that sustain that tradition in contemporary conditions. But I value St Benedict's principle that the day should embrace work, prayer and study. And even if I live in the material world with a family, a job and temporal responsibilities, I try to reach to the contemplative values that are to be realised in the non-material world.

I value reflection, even though I am not very skilled at it. There is something very wonderful about the pause for silent prayer and meditation that comes in the middle of the Cistercian/Benedictine *lectio divina*. I am never unmoved by the experience of sitting silently with others, in a dedicated space, seeking to reach God. And I like the idea that there are men and women whose daily purpose is to come together at fixed times simply to give praise to their Creator.

Of course other faiths and other churches present various options to their members in seeking to identify ways of expressing their spirituality. But I do not believe that any of them offer quite the range and variety that the Catholic Church provides.

I also value the continuity and the consistency of Catholic principles and fundamental teachings: the mystery of the Trinity; the miracle of the Eucharist; the Communion of Saints; the forgiveness of sins; the promise of eternal life; the power of prayer. These are unchanging over two thousand years. It has been said that if the Christian Churches generally are 'the anchor of faith,' the Catholic Church is the 'anchor of history'.

I value these teachings and this continuity – for all that I grieve at the failures in practice, the myopia, the self-serving defensiveness, the cowardice that have characterised so many actions and decisions and positions that have been set down by the Church's authorities.

I have two children now in their twenties. It is not easy to convince them of the essential goodness of the Catholic Church against a background of child abuse, exploitation, cover-up and hypocrisy over many decades here in their own country. And I find myself increasingly asking myself do I really have the commitment and the conviction any longer that mark me as a member of the Catholic faith?

A high-profile convert to Catholicism during the 1970s said that he had embraced Catholicism because it was the only faith that gave him all the necessary supports, guidance and answers that he required. He was describing a sort of 'one stop shop' for the spiritual life. I would argue that, however dire the circumstances in which the human spirit may find itself, the Catholic faith presents a framework, a range of sacramental 'supports' and a set of truths that for me, at least, can make some sense of the mysteries of existence.

If I still have that faith – and at this stage it is faith, rather than an intellectual conviction – it is a gift from God. Others have been given different gifts and those gifts may have brought them to their own, particular spiritual destiny. But I have been given my Catholic faith as my gift. I embrace it as such – and I know that I am fortunate.

On the Brink of the Abyss?

Brendan Ryan

I'm not sure anymore what it all means, though I am sure about the pretty scary void that might open in my life if I were to abandon it. I hasten to add that, however scary it may be, the void I fear is utterly unconnected with any fear of eternal damnation or any such like vision. It is rather a sense of loss more familiar to philosophers and poets than to a touch-and-feel engineer like myself. It is well summed up by Mathew Arnold in 'Dover Beach' when he says:

> The Sea of Faith
> Was once, too, at the full, and round earth's shore
> Lay like the folds of a bright girdle furled.
> But now I only hear
> Its melancholy, long, withdrawing roar,
> Retreating, to the breath
> Of the night wind, down the vast edges drear
> And naked shingles of the world.

But while it is real, and perhaps is what comes most easily to mind, fear of 'the void' is by no means the most profound or the most compelling reason for holding on. Indeed it would be a very dishonest and far from courageous way to live.

There are many more positive and deep rooted reasons. However, coming upon those, and even more so writing about them, seems to have more to do with the experience of Zen than of routine religious practice. In other words, if you search too explicitly for them they disappear from view. I am certain of the value for me and for the world of continuing religious practice (and something that is best called, if very inadequately and for want of a better word, faith). I am certain that it contributes to my deep sense of the value of living, the joy it still contains, the vibrant sense of expectation for the future, the sense of continuing infinite possibilities, the continuing sense of mystery and the urgency of the need for profound change in our values. But I am not sure how that sense and the insights that convey it infiltrate my life.

The insights come at you when you least expect them, rarely when you sit and meditate in the recommended quiet space. They come from the world vision of a very dear and very atheistic (and currently very distant) friend. They come from a sideways respect for the rigour and, perhaps paradoxically, the wrongness of much of my Church's attempt at intellectual analysis of the modern world. And they come from an acute sense of a strange and mostly hidden providence that seems, provided you don't go trying to look for it, to shape our lives. And as well they come from art, music, human love in all its forms and, of course, nature. They sneak up on you though; sometimes they ambush you.

It is often a 3.00am feeling, a need for calmness in the face of personal, political and other pressures. The techniques that bring about the calmness are secular as much as spiritual, and they often work and calmness descends. But in the calmness an invitation to the Lord often produces the utterly ambiguous experience that John Updike once talked about. A sense of something so gentle that you could never even say with any certainty that it happened, but a sense too when you look back at it days later, perhaps in a time of strife or pain, that Someone seems to reach through time and space and heal.

I'm not sure that that is what is called a faith experience but it is without a doubt an experience and one that seems to me not to be capable of any convincing alternative explanation.

But that deep rich and often healing experience comes wrapped with more than a little pain. The pain touches at a more superficial level admittedly but its presence is more constant and more ubiquitous than the delightful deep but often transitory healing and joy. Most of that pain comes from outside, and on my outside is the Church through which I endeavour to maintain my ambiguous faith. It is a long time since I felt like an insider in my Church. And it's not getting better.

Today I feel the pain of an outsider more than ever before. There are many reasons for the pain. Some are doctrinal (not only am I 'à la carte' I sometimes suspect that my 'carte' belongs in a different restaurant altogether!) and many more are related to the practice of those who claim the right to tell me what I must do. None are related directly to the obvious things like the sinfulness which was in the lives of some who claimed to have dedicated their lives to the Lord. Sinful clergy are nothing new in our Church after all, nor indeed are sinful popes. It is dreadful that some priests and religious abused children in the way that they did. But the clerical Church was never any more immune from sinfulness than the rest of us. That much was clear to most lay people for most of the last two thousand years. Only the dominant clerical Church has tried and continues to try to pretend otherwise. What else can one say about the hierarchy of titles from 'Reverend' (loosely translated as 'requiring to be revered') through 'His Grace', to 'His Eminence' and finally 'His Holiness'? That heavily emphasised sense of a superior (male) lifestyle apart from the rest of us is part of all our experiences. And, of course, that same self-congratulatory clerical Church never quite accepted that true holiness was possible for those who lived normal healthy married lives, those who celebrated all the joys and all the struggles of lasting and successful human love. The clerical Church far preferred saints to be virgins or widows or hermits or priests. In other words, they preferred people much like themselves. Normality, living as God intended us to live, was not until recently a widely proclaimed route to sanctity. There are still few enough saints who celebrated the joy of human love in marriage, who loved being married, and who joyfully shared the love of a woman or a man through their lifetime. What does one say to the millions of mothers who saw a woman canonised because she decided to refuse perfectly moral medical treatment thereby preserving the life of an unborn child and by that decision depriving other children of the love, care and protection of a mother?

There is nothing new in all of this. But the genuine liberation of the past forty years has enabled us to talk about it. And many of us found that, as we talked, the enormity of the distortion became more and more obvious. It is obvious in the exclusion of women from all the instruments of power in the Church. That used to be explained away with a trite 'service not power' one liner but no one (outside the clerical Church) believes that anymore. But even that universal and oppressive subjection of women was no more than a symptom of something much deeper. Deeper was a profound and hugely negative perception of human sexuality. This, of course, is denied with even more vehemence than the denial of the oppression of women. And yet as we began to talk about sex over the past forty years a fundamental question arose for me, one that put me far away from what calls itself the Magisterium. The question is not about the abuse of sexuality, nor the commercialisation of sexuality, nor the degradation of women by pornography, nor about the dreadful commercially driven sexualisation of our children. On all these issues there is genuine reason to be concerned and a real need for a sense of genuine humanist morality. My question is much simpler. It is about the Magisterium view that virtually all sexual acts which are deemed to be wrong, like extra marital sex, or masturbation, or homosexual acts, or sex between married couples whose birth control methods do not meet with Church approval, are deemed to be as serious in the eyes of the Lord as murder. There may be a spectrum of horror but in each case the gravity of the act is deemed sufficient to merit separation from the Lord forever.

And on that I will not serve! I cannot accept that the current lifestyles of most of our young people, nor the practices of mature adults who choose not to marry nor of those who for one reason or another cannot marry but who have active and responsible sexual lives, nor the practices of homosexual couples, are evil in the eyes of the Lord in the way that murder, rape or child abuse are. I cannot accept, as some in the clerical Church have suggested, that there is a moral equivalence between the offence of Bishop Eamon Casey and that of our too numerous clerical child rapists. Only a morbidly obsessive mind could suggest that. As I grow older (and perhaps more than a little envious of younger people!) I wonder more and more how our Church came to force something so potentially joyous, liberating and life-affirming into a box which was labelled 'explosive, dangerous and a threat to your religious faith'. Sex can be abused, as can every other good thing that God gave us. How a morality evolved which put sexual acts up there with acts of violence and cruelty and murder in terms of their gravity deserves both study, reflection and, in my view, wholehearted apology from the clerical Church. That morbid obsessive fear and revulsion foisted upon us by a clerical Church I think I have escaped, but the escape means that in my heart I am a long way from a Church which imposed such a scandalous burden of guilt, isolation and pain on so many of us.

Apologies are things our Church is not good at. They are usually carefully worded and cautiously and coldly constrained. Archbishop Brady spoke to the Polish bishops in 2004. He explained the decline in religious practice in Ireland as being partly caused by 'the perception' that clerical child sexual abuse was badly handled. But of course it wasn't a 'perception' – it was a fact that the issue was handled appallingly. It is the fact that needs to be analysed, and apologised for, not the perception of the laity. When the diocese of Cloyne hit the headlines we were told that people 'feel let down'. Again it wasn't a feeling; it was a fact that people were let down.

I am aware of many apologies for 'mistakes' from the hierarchical Church, many of them I am sure deeply felt and wholehearted. I am not, however, aware of any major words or acts of penitence by the self-same hierarchical Church. And of course the difference is clear. Mistakes are just that, mistakes. Mistakes are regrettable, but they sometimes arise out of ignorance, lack of experience or some other deficit for which there can be no personal or group culpability. Wrong-doing is different. Protecting child rapists so as to 'avoid scandal' (weasel words for protecting the institution) is not a mistake, it is serious wrong-doing and sinful. And for all of us Christians forgiveness of sin demands repentance. So far little or no repentance has been visible in our Magisterium. It is the collective view of our hierarchy that a woman who uses a forbidden method of birth control is more culpable in the eyes of the Lord than a bishop or religious superior who protected and covered up for a child rapist. For many of the laity the offence of Bishop Casey was infinitely less significant in the eyes of the Lord than that of those of his 'brother' bishops who left children at risk in order to 'avoid scandal'. And piled onto all that we now have the revelations of the Ryan Report, the equivocation of many religious, and the apparent determination of the Catholic hierarchy to point the finger at the religious. From 1922 to the late 1970s in the areas of health, education, childcare, and family values generally, Ireland ran the way the bishops wanted it to run. Church power was absolute and the state and its institutions capitulated. The Ireland of that era was presented to the world as a model of Christian society. For many, those are still the good old days. For many others those days are the final reason to walk away. Only those of us who are cross, cussed, concerned or cowed will stay on. I stay and I get mad.

But, of course, if I didn't care I wouldn't get so mad. Spiritual values are so much at the centre of our lives, are enriching and are utterly necessary. Yet the most visible, the most tangible, revelation of those values is separated from many of our people and from most of our young people by the shame of recent years and the morbid obsessions of centuries.

What a glorious thing Christian faith can be. Glorious, positive, life-affirming, and enriching. Christian faith renews all parts of our lives. It deepens the impact of music in our lives, it enriches the beauty of the visual in art and in nature and it offers us a capacity to understand and live values like 'enough' and 'moderation'. It enhances our friendships, our families and (dare I say it) our love affairs.

But, of course, it does more. It opens our spirit to the revelation of God, our God of Love, our God of Freedom. Surely that is the message of Jesus Christ, that love is real and possible, that we humans uniquely among living creatures are capable of and regularly practise genuine altruistic love, not for reasons of sexual desire, parental instinct or DNA linkages but because we choose in freedom to do it. It has always seemed to me that real love is not possible without real freedom. And that is the gift God has given us, the gift of really being able to make acts of love. Such love can enrich families, can enrich sexual love and parental love, but it is a form of love over and beyond all that. It is a love based on choices freely made and freely sustained. It is the love of Martin Luther King, Helder Camara, Oscar Romero, Dorothy Day or indeed Nelson Mandela. It is the love of the huge numbers of people who opt for (often poorly paid) work in the 'caring' professions, just as it is the love of those who accept and live a genuinely religious vocation. It is also the love that is often so beautifully visible between old people long after desire (and often desirability!) has faded. It is love grounded on the glory of human freedom and knowledge that we can and often do choose to love. And for me, it is the revelation of God.

For many like me, that amounts to a painful paradox. We learn about real love and real freedom through the best side of an institution. But in that learning we are forced to confront an abuse of power so endemic that its practitioners can even deny power exists at all. We are forced too to confront a vision of human sexuality which is so distorted, so overlain with fear and repression, and so at variance with human experience, as to merit the term 'perversion'. We respond to this confrontation in different ways. It is enough to cause many, quite reasonably, to move out and away and seek meaning elsewhere. It is the painful experience of adult Christians that many of the best people we know have long moved away from any physical or even spiritual link with the Church. Sometimes I envy them but rarely for long. I have the good (or mis)fortune to have learned how to move beyond all that while remaining within the institution. So, to misrepresent Martin Luther completely, 'Here I stand and I can do no other.' And then there is always Thomas Merton!

The Cracks in my Catholicism

Garry O'Sullivan

The first expectation of people upon meeting the editor of a Catholic newspaper is that he or she must be a 'holy Joe'. I never get tired of disabusing people of this cliché and thrive on challenging them as to why they would think such a thing. Does a sports editor need to be a great athlete and so on? Perhaps it is because people don't associate an interest in religion/spirituality with everyday pursuits: it's for the priests, the religious, the elite, the geeks, the humourless, the saintly, and the needy.

Yet, when asked, people admit they are 'spiritual', so they are not completely removed from the world of religion, though they often see it that way. It is as if there are spiritual people and then religious people, the latter who perform the outward rituals of religion and the former who don't. This dichotomy between faith as an interiorised emotion and faith as an exterior practice is a sickness eating away at Christianity. There is little understanding of life being a journey to becoming more fully human, that we're on a spiritual quest and that it is all part of the same end game; there is no dichotomy.

As a post-Vatican II child, I live in the no-man's land that exists now in the Irish Church between old Irish Catholicism, anti-Irish Catholicism and a new Irish Catholicism in embryonic stage – we are in transition but lost in translation. Perhaps a better name for it is the limbo generation. Let me explain if I can by letting you in on a little of my own journey.

In our offices in *The Irish Catholic* we have one framed reproduction of Caravaggio's *Supper at Emmaus*. The story of the disciples on the road to Emmaus is probably the best metaphoric description of my own personal journey as a Catholic Christian.

The revelation at Emmaus (and on the road) was a recalling from confusion and disenchantment to the joy of the Gospel. The road to Emmaus from Jerusalem was one road among many. The disciples had experienced the idealism of following Christ on the road to Jerusalem with all its piety, naïvety, simplicity, joyfulness and camaraderie, childlike in their understanding of parables and unable to see the bigger movements at play. When the journey ended in Jerusalem, the reality of it all hit home. At Passover, the followers were concerned, bewildered and in the shadow of the cross, filled with fear and trepidation and understandable cowardice. Even when Christ rose from the dead, some couldn't believe it and many who believed it couldn't understand it. They hid despite Christ's resurrection. The Acts of the Apostles illustrates this with Peter and the early Christian-Jews grappling with understanding the true extent of God's plan, and their own on-going conversion and reluctance, as St Augustine so aptly put that feeling – 'not yet Lord, not yet'. My own story, then, is one of struggle, one that identifies with the grittiness of the Gospel and the failures and successes of the disciples to follow Christ faithfully. Perhaps most prominently has been the persistent questioning and doubt – faith seeking understanding – I am a seeker.

As a teenager growing up in Wicklow I developed an interest in spirituality and especially Franciscanism. I'm not sure where it came from but it certainly wasn't from school.

The idealism of the Gospel was compelling, especially the stories of Jesus in Galilee and the 'adventures' of the disciples during those three years of public ministry.

For me it was easy to see why St Francis of Assisi was compelled by the romanticism of following Jesus and why he threw away all earthly cares and abandoned himself to God. Reading the stories of his own travels (*The Little Flowers*) along the plains of Umbria, those tales shone with bright summer sunshine, meadows of flowers, medieval castles and heroic exploits, enough to capture the heart and idealism of an eighteen year old.

I didn't want to be a priest, but I was interested in the missions. The 'ordinary' Franciscans were not enough for my youthful idealism; I determined that only the most reformed branch of the Franciscans whose lives were closest to the first followers of St Francis would be good enough for me. I discovered the Capuchins and their big church on Church Street in Dublin and the Day Centre they ran for homeless people. They were real, down to earth, bearded and seemed very happy. It was very real but also scary, yet I wanted the adventure, so I joined with my parents' blessing.

My almost four years in the Capuchins were very happy though the last year was belaboured with doubts. I'll never forget the words of a daily Mass goer to me in front of the friary one day when word had gone around that I was leaving: 'Brother, I heard you're leaving. Well many are called but few are chosen.' It was a reminder of the nasty old days when men who were brave enough to take responsibility for their lives were labelled 'spoilt priests'.

No amount of hand-bagging by old ladies could have changed my mind. I was and I am convinced I didn't have a vocation.

After religious life I worked in a variety of jobs until I was accepted into DCU and did a degree in Communications followed by a Master's in Journalism. I worked for *The Irish Voice* in New York for a year followed by a year as a producer and presenter in Vatican Radio in Rome. I spent two years as a full-time journalist with *The Irish Catholic* as well as editing *The Word* magazine, and during 2002 wrote most of the *Irish Independent*'s editorials and a lot of their opinion editorials on the child abuse crisis. I then took a job with the Jesuits as their Communications Manager and spent a very enjoyable two years with them.

However, after six months looking for a suitable editor, *The Irish Catholic* and I got into a discussion: they were keen to modernise the paper to combat a new start-up which was posing a real threat. I sought assurances that the modernisation wasn't just going to be cosmetic. As I saw it, whether we as Catholics liked it or not, we had either to flow out with the tide and negotiate the waves of secularism or be left stranded on the beach talking to ourselves or, more likely, fighting among ourselves. It's been a tightrope act ever since.

So what does being a Catholic mean to me now? Being a Catholic means being a liberal, a conservative, a progressive, a traditionalist, a heathen, a Jew and a Greek.

It means having the strength to follow my own path, to take responsibility for my life and to be led by my conscience. We are spiritual beings on a spiritual quest and we have to be true to that, which is rarely easy.

I also think being a Catholic today means actively finding out more about the Church and what it teaches and why it teaches it. The Pope has said that we must talk about the faith as a positive option and not as a list of negatives. So many people see the Church as anything but positive and, backed by a negative experience, walk away.

And that said, there is a huge laziness among the vast majority of people to take some responsibility for their personal spiritual journey. They may even be regular Mass goers but the understanding of the faith is very poor. Perhaps only when Christianity on this island is really threatened with de facto extinction – like during the Penal times – will the necessary catechetical reforms be implemented which will teach people about dynamic spirituality.

Being Catholic in Ireland today means not being listened to. I've been the editor of Ireland's largest Catholic newspaper for four years and never have been asked by a bishop for an opinion or even invited for a cup of tea. Archbishop Diarmuid Martin sent his solicitors after me over a reader's letter he didn't like, which sums up the episcopal tolerance for robust criticism.

I can understand that there is huge fear of media among clergy. Yet the Church in Ireland has gone backwards since Vatican II in its approach to communications. Every year the Bishops' Conference will pontificate about communications in the Church, they'll put up videos about it on its website and welcome the Pope's letter for world communications day. But letters from laity and priests often don't get answered, opportunities for transparency, dialogue and understanding get lost, as the general policy seems to be why go out the front door when you can go out the back (and I can think of two bishops' meetings in Maynooth when they did just that to avoid the waiting media). I don't lose sleep over this, but I lament the impoverishment of the Church's communications because it's the ordinary people who have suffered as a result. They have turned their backs and walked away from the Church; people who could be persuaded by a kind word or a bit of decency. Jesus fretted over the lost sheep, the prodigal son, and yet here in Ireland we lose them in their thousands, like water trickling through our fingers because of an unwillingness to embrace dynamic communications which should be at the heart of how the Church and its leadership do business. If laypeople with professional competence in certain areas are not consulted or even spoken to in order to gain expertise, is it any wonder that the communications of the Irish bishops has been a disaster (and we're seeing similar problems in the Vatican now). It has taken twenty years to get child protection policies right; could that not have been done more quickly had the Church leadership listened to the wisdom of the laity instead of trusting in their own ability to sort it out?

But it's not all negative. Being Catholic today has the potential to be very positive. Firstly there isn't the oppressiveness of the past, and people can take it or leave it. The expression 'à la carte' Catholic is thrown around – we love labels in the Catholic Church – but what it means is young people can experiment with their faith on a voyage of discovery. I always believed that Jesus tried to give his disciples an experience of God first, and then the rest fell into place. Conversely, we try to instil the rules and regulations first and if the experience of God comes later on then all the better but it's not guaranteed and no one is going to show you how anyway.

Being Catholic today means rediscovering community – we can't find Christ on our own (that's why Jesus always spoke about finding the lost sheep), we all stray and need the strength and understanding and compassion of community. Many parishes are alive, many have great priests and many dioceses have wonderful bishops. Many laity could not care less about Church structures, they just want a good priest so that they can bring their kids along on Sunday to Mass and have support in times of need.

The Jesuits have a catchphrase – 'Finding God in all things'. Perhaps that is how we should see being Catholic today – after all *catholic* means *universal*. It could be a Catholic logo for our age. It is a tragedy that in Ireland the word Catholic has come to be seen as narrow-minded, right-wing and intellectually impoverished. Being Catholic, being Christian, should mean the opposite of all of these.

John Moriarty, the philosopher and mystic from Kerry who died two years ago, once said, 'I wonder if we will have to follow Christ out of Christianity?' It may be that we have to follow Christ out of Irish Catholicism or what passed for Christianity in Ireland. This was eloquently put by poet Brendan Kennelly when he said, 'The problem with Christianity in Ireland is that it has never been tried.'

If the limbo generations have been failed by this version of Christianity, then the Church needs to listen very carefully; it may be that it as institution, like the prodigal son's older brother, is also in need of evangelisation.

The line from the gospels that appeals to me most is, 'I came that you may have life and have it to the full.' I don't believe Jesus was solely talking about eternal life – why have a Garden of Eden if paradise was to be found elsewhere? Ultimately we live with great mystery and my vision for Catholicism in Ireland is rediscovering some of the mystery and leaving behind the infallibility and the moral righteousness. Behind all the arrogance and hubris of some priests, religious and laity in the past lay a huge cancerous sore, and thank God it has been lanced. There was Anti-Christ in the Irish Catholic Church and Irish society – how else would you describe the most heinous crimes against children, and there are not enough millstones in the world to punish all the perpetrators.

Being Catholic today means also, and this is hard, carrying the cross of the past and allowing it to be a source of humility to us all. Those who abused were the sons and daughters of civil servants, farmers, gardaí and so on and came from good families. Being Catholic today means having the patience to wait for better leadership in the Church, to hope to be listened to someday, to listen to the faint sound of the Holy Spirit among us as a community and in the depths of our own very troubled, conflicted, and cracked human hearts. We need to embrace our faults, our failings, our brokenness and learn compassion for ourselves and for others, for it is often those who are most broken who enter the kingdom first

Being Catholic today means holding in tension, like the cross, our longing and thirst for divinity like the vertical beam which comes up from the ground and reaches up into the sky, crossed by our brokenness, like the horizontal beam, which pulls us away in other directions from that ascent. It all belongs; neither is right nor wrong nor can be divorced from the other. We cannot divorce our humanity from our longing for divinity or vice versa or repress one over the other. When we do, we get the Inquisition or the Reign of Terror. The good thief and the bad thief are the flip side of each other, everything belongs, darkness and light.

What it Means to Me to Be a Catholic

William Reville

I always felt that there is more to the totality of things than can be explained by material causes alone and my scientific under-standing of the world reinforces that feeling. So, the spiritual dimension is important to me and the spiritual family to which I belong is the Catholic Church. The fact that I am both a scientist and a Catholic requires me to clarify my thoughts on the rela-tionship between science and religion, a theme I will develop in this chapter.

Early years

I was born into the Catholic faith in New Ross, Co. Wexford. I received my primary and secondary education at New Ross Christian Brothers School in the 1950/1960s and I also served as an altar boy in the Augustinian church. My early experiences with the Church were happy, although I witnessed some exces-sive corporal punishment in school. Being a Catholic then largely seemed to mean carrying out rituals in a fairly unreflective man-ner, but I was content to go with the flow.

I did well at school, a performance significantly encouraged by several of my teachers. Some of the Christian Brothers had petty habits but, by and large, they seemed to be fine men. I al-ways felt they lead isolated and unnecessarily constricted lives – I leafed through their rule-book one day when sent on an errand to the monastery.

I won a Wexford County Council open university scholar-ship based on my Leaving Certificate results. I was under the impression that science was 'the coming thing', and I liked the subject, so I went to UCD to study science. I graduated with a

BSc, and a PhD in Biochemistry in 1973, and then I undertook research in muscle biology as a Fulbright Scholar at Iowa State University until August 1975. We (I married Breda McLeavey in 1972) returned to Ireland and I got a job at UCC, where I have worked since as Professor of Biochemistry, College Radiation Protection Officer and Public Awareness of Science Officer. I also write the weekly science column in *The Irish Times* and public promotion of science now occupies much of my time.

What science has discovered about the world

Over the past five hundred years science has discovered the most amazing knowledge about the physical world, and modern civilisation is absolutely dependent on the technological applications of this knowledge. We know that the world began at a single point about fourteen billion years ago in a massive explosion called the Big Bang. The universe has been expanding outwards ever since. We know how the stars formed, and later the planets. We know how the ninety-two natural elements were made – the two lightest, hydrogen and helium, were made in the Big Bang and the remaining ninety were bred later inside stars. The human body is based on carbon and every atom of carbon in your body was made in a star.

We know how our solar system formed about five billion years ago. We know in principle how life began on earth about 3.8 billion years ago as a single simple form. We know how life evolved from that simple origin eventually to produce the myriad forms that today colonise every environmental niche on earth. We understand the four fundamental forces that determine everything physical that happens – gravity, electromagnetism and the strong and weak nuclear forces.

We understand the large scale structure of the universe and we can predict the future of the universe. For example, we know that in five billion years' time our sun will die and life will no longer be possible on earth. And we know that, in the almost unimaginably distant future, the entire universe will be reduced to a frozen barren wasteland when all of the stars have died.

Science and religion are not fundamentally opposed to one another
Science can explain how the physical world bootstrapped its way from pure energy in the Big Bang up to me writing this article, without any need to invoke supernatural assistance. This explanation does not rule out the possibility of a Creator but it does require that, if there is a Creator, he made a world capable of developing 'under its own steam'. However, as I will explain later, some detailed considerations reveal that more may be going on behind the scientific scene than first meets the eye.

In my public promotion of science, I occasionally deal with the relationship between science and religion, which always excites great interest Many people think that science and religion are fundamentally at odds and that atheism and agnosticism are the only tenable positions for a scientist. They are wrong.

The function of science is to discover the natural mechanisms that underpin the natural world. Science cannot invoke supernatural mechanisms. Science is naturalistic, or materialistic, in its method of investigation but not in its philosophy. Science neither affirms nor denies the supernatural – it simply has nothing to say about it.

You don't have to adopt a materialistic philosophy to be a scientist. Many scientists are materialistic atheists, but forty per cent of scientists believe in God. Historically most of the greatest scientists were devout Christians, for example, Galileo Galilei (1564-1642), Johannes Kepler (1571-1630), Isaac Newton (1643-1727), Gregor Mendel (1822-1884), Louis Pasteur (1822-1895) and so on. This tradition continues today, for example, the renowned evolutionary biologists Theodosius Dobzhansky (1900-1975), Simon Conway Morris (1951-) and Francis Collins (1950-). Personally, I see no conflict between accepting all that science discovers and being a Christian.

Christianity provided fertile ground in which science took root
In fact a reasonable case can be made that science would never have arisen but for Christianity. True science began in fifteenth century Christian Europe – why only here and not, for example,

in China or Greece, or under Islam? The Chinese culture concentrated on personal enlightenment and never expected that a 'science of explanations' would be possible. The Greeks pursued speculative ideas but believed in a world influenced by many fallible gods. Islam made progress in mathematics, astronomy and medicine but was much influenced by the classical Greek view of an inscrutable universe, which blocked further progress.

On the other hand, Christians believe in a rational lawgiving God who created the world according to his nature and in which this nature is displayed for our benefit and instruction. The Christian would expect the world to be understandable and would feel not only compelled to study it in order to understand the mind of God, but also free to do so because the creation, unlike God, is not itself divine. This argument has been well made by several authors in recent times, such as Rodney Stark in his book *The Victory of Reason* (Random House, 2006).

Some scientific considerations of the universe
point towards the possibility of a designer-God
Although science has nothing directly to say about the supernatural, nevertheless some scientific considerations of the universe raise questions to which God is a possible answer. One such question relates to the comprehensibility of the world, and another to implications arising from the anthropic principle.

Albert Einstein said: 'The only thing I find incomprehensible about the universe is the fact that it is comprehensible.' Science explains how the universe works and the language of science is written in mathematics. Mathematics is a product of the human imagination – basically it is pattern formation. The mathematician sits alone, thinks up new ways to form patterns and expresses these patterns as equations. Then when the mathematician looks out the window he/she finds that these equations are already out there written into the basic fabric of the universe.

This is a striking coincidence. In the words of the Anglican priest-scientist John Polkinghorne, 'It is as if the universe is shot through with mind.' Christians believe we are made in the image of God and therefore our minds dimly resemble the mind of God. So, the fact that we can comprehend the universe may simply reflect our capacity to recognise the creative workings of a mind similar to our own.

The anthropic principle (AP) is a scientific principle introduced by Brandon Carter in 1973. It simply states that any scientific consideration of the universe must accommodate the fact of the presence of intelligent observers. Thus, for example, the AP explains why the universe has to be about fourteen billion years old – because it takes that long after the Big Bang for all the elements essential for life to be formed in stars and then for life to begin and slowly evolve to eventually produce intelligent observers.

Other considerations arising from the AP draw attention to the values of fundamental physical constants in our universe, like the charge on the electron, the cosmological constant, and so on. Calculations show that, if the values of these constants were ever so slightly different from the values that they have, and as far as we understand things these values could have fallen out differently, life would either never have arisen on earth or else it would not have evolved into anything interesting. For example, if the force of gravity were slightly stronger, stars would burn too rapidly to allow life-supporting conditions on surrounding planets.

The possibility therefore arises that the universe is fine-tuned for life. In the words of the noted physicist John Freeman Dyson, 'It's as though the universe knew we were coming.' It may well be that, as Fred Hoyle, the astronomer who worked out many of the details of how the elements are bred in the stars, believed, the world is 'rigged' at its quantum roots to allow developments that favour the origin and evolution of life.

Can belief in a personal God be reasonable?
Although the scientific considerations I have described constitute no more than a finger pointing vaguely towards the possibility of God, nevertheless, a rational case can be made for Deism,

that is, that the world was designed by a super- intelligence. But what about a personal God such as Catholics are required to believe in? Many people argue that such a belief is not reasonable for a scientist because it requires an act of faith. Faith here is interpreted as belief in the absence of evidence. But this is not how I understand faith. To me, any faith that insults reason is a useless thing, but I believe that it can be reasonable to believe in the personal God of Christianity under the following conditions.

Jesus Christ claimed to be in constant communication with a God who created the world, who loves us and wants us to live according to his teachings. If you believe that Jesus Christ was sane, if his teachings stake a claim on your heart and your head, if you find that living by these principles brings you peace and joy, then it is as reasonable for you to take the word of Jesus about the God he spoke of as it is to take the word of any tried and trusted friend about a matter of which you have no direct personal experience.

Clashes between science and religion

The clash between Galileo (1564-1642) and the Church is often quoted to illustrate the 'inevitable' clash between science and religion. However, it now seems clear that this affair was more complex than portrayed in the conventional account. Galileo was asking a lot – no less than the immediate overthrow of the whole Aristotelian thought system, a system not only deeply embedded in the Church but also in general academic circles. This was also a dangerous time to challenge ecclesiastical authority since the church was under siege from the Reformation. Galileo was offered a compromise by the Church – teach the heliocentric model as a hypothesis until proof of the model became available, but he did not accept this compromise. Nevertheless, of course, the Church was wrong to oppose Galileo's scientific findings, wrong to bring him to trial, and grievously wrong to trump up false evidence against him.

Another frequently quoted illustration of the clash between science and religion is the resistance mounted by the Church to the theory of evolution by natural selection introduced by Darwin and Wallace in 1858. The story is often told with relish of the clash between Samuel Wilberforce, Bishop of Oxford, and Thomas Huxley, defender of the theory of evolution, at a meeting of the British Association in Oxford in 1860 when Darwin's new theory was debated. Wilberforce made a scathing attack on the new theory and then sneeringly asked of Huxley, 'Is it through your grandfather or your grandmother that you claim descent from a monkey?' Huxley replied, 'I am not ashamed to have a monkey for my ancestor, but I would be ashamed to be connected with a man who used his great gifts to obscure the truth.'

This is a good story, but it never happened. People who attended the meeting could not recall this scintillating interchange and official reports of the meeting do not record it. In fact Wilberforce is recorded to have made a learned criticism of Darwin's ideas. Darwin took pains to deal with Wilberforce's arguments in subsequent editions of *The Origin of Species*.

Darwin and Wallace pretty much demolished the then universally accepted explanation of the origin of species as described in the Book of Genesis – God created the world about six thousand years ago in six days; he created the biological species individually and in the same form in which we see them today; finally he created the first two humans, Adam and Eve, and placed them at the pinnacle of the created world.

Darwin's theory completely contradicts Genesis. It assumes that life spontaneously arose on earth billions of years ago and slowly developed into innumerable species, including humans, who colonise every environmental niche on earth today. Humans arose very recently in evolutionary history when the hominid line branched off from the ape line several million years ago.

Naturally this new radical explanation for life on earth was initially greeted with shock by the Christian Churches. However, mainline Christianity quickly came to terms with evolution and, today, only a minority of fundamentalist Christians reject evolution. The Catholic Church has no objection to the theory of evolution as an explanation of the physical origin of species, including man. The creation account in Genesis is now accepted as a story with a moral message. However, while the Church gives science the body it reserves the soul for God, holding that its introduction into the human body is a divine intervention. Science, as always, has nothing to say about the soul.

The current situation

Coming right up to date, I agree with the Catholic Church that human life begins at conception and therefore I am opposed to human embryonic stem cell research, and to abortion, which destroys the embryo. My understanding of when human life begins is based on biology, the science of life, which clearly tells us that life begins at conception, the start of the development of life between the two boundaries of conception and death. When a sperm unites with an egg, a zygote is formed, the first embryonic stage. This grows and develops successively into a foetus, baby, adult, elderly person and the continuum ends in death. Each point on the continuum has the properties and capacities appropriate to its stage and each is fully human and deserving of the respect appropriate to humanity. The right not to be deliberately killed is surely the minimum level of such respect.

There are other areas, however, where I cannot agree with the Catholic Church, for example on the issues of artificial contraception and in-vitro fertilisation (IVF). I do not see the moral wrong in a married couple using artificial contraception sensibly to space their children's births, or using contraception later on when they have agreed not to conceive any more children. Likewise I have no problem with a married couple resorting to IVF, having failed to conceive a child after extensive efforts using natural conventional means, although I do not favour IVF methods that generate 'spare embryos' destined to be destroyed eventually.

Finally, I am saddened at the present position of the Catholic Church in Ireland. The recent revelations about the sexual and physical abuse of defenceless young people in institutions by brothers and sisters while under their care have been devastating. The Catholic Church is deeply shamed by these events, where many of its members in Holy Orders behaved in such an anti-Christian manner. The initial reaction of the Church to these and other shocking revelations was less than frank.

The Irish Catholic Church is now reaping the rewards of long decades of standing on a pedestal having its backside kissed by a passive and compliant laity, while interpreting its mission as the enforcement of ritualised obligations, an interpretation quite at variance with the spirit of the founder Jesus Christ. Any institution that behaves in this manner will inevitably grow lazy, arrogant and, in parts at least, corrupt. When the Church seemed strongest in Ireland it was actually very weak. The universal practice of the faith gave a false impression of robust health. In fact this 'faith' had very shallow roots. The recent scandals have undoubtedly lessened the practice of the Catholic faith in Ireland, but I am convinced that this practice would have declined anyway because much of our faith was too weakly rooted in free personal conviction to withstand the onslaught of our new affluence. The future of the Catholic Church in Ireland depends on how well and how soon it returns to its roots – the teachings of Jesus Christ.

Beyond Legalism – A Philosophy of Life

Thomas Finegan

Ireland, as an historical and geographical entity, is not essentially Catholic. Nowhere is. Yet it is fair to say that the current traject-ories within Irish culture are largely – though by no means ex-clusively – away from its Catholic heritage. Quite a few com-mentators would see this as a cathartic reaction against a once dominant, and too often controlling, patriarchal institution. Yet it is at least as plausible that in some cases it is a genuine rejec-tion of mystery, selflessness and transcendence. Some of these movements in our cultural milieu are becoming more overtly in-tolerant of Catholicism, and not just 'institutional Catholicism', but of the Catholic faith itself. This by itself is barely a value judgement, for tolerance is a minimalist virtue. This intolerance is evident from various strands of Irish public life such as the activities of certain political advocacy groups and the ideology underpinning the mainstream media (especially the twin pillars of *The Irish Times* and RTÉ). But it is important to understand that this intolerance is aimed more at the philosophical content of Catholicism rather than at an individual Catholic's right to freedom of religion.

Indeed, freedom from constraints to both religious practice and education – at both public and private levels – and the right to conscientious objection, are still relatively well safeguarded in the jurisdiction of Ireland in comparison to, for example, Britain. Key issues that are constantly under close public scrutiny are the extent to which Catholic-inspired ideals are incorporated in the creation of a just society, and also the extent to which society takes seriously the religious dimension to human existence. What makes these issues especially difficult to approach from a

Catholic perspective is the well-documented abuse of young children by Catholic clergy and religious congregations through-out the twentieth century. As a young Catholic writing in the aftermath of the Ryan Report and in expectation of the Arch-diocese of Dublin report into child abuse, these are testing times for my own faith convictions, even if I am too young to be implicated in the violence that took place at the hands of sup-posed Catholic leaders and exemplars.

It may seem a little out of place to begin my contribution by referencing the general cultural and political climate in which I find myself. But, like almost all dichotomies, the public/personal version has little by way of rational justification. Personal faith of whatever kind is an existential response to the world one is, to borrow a term from Martin Heidegger, 'thrown' into. Faith is al-ways personal, but ought never to be a solely private matter. My own faith journey began in a household nominally and procedur-ally Catholic, but sometimes lacking in the authentic spiritual dimension inherent in the best of religion. My teenage years were a gradual cooling off of religious interest in inverse pro-portion to greater immersion in the worlds of sport and socialis-ing. This changed somewhat when, just days before I was due to begin an accountancy course in Dublin City University (DCU), I broke and dislocated my ankle playing football for my local GAA club, Wolfetones of Co. Meath.

What followed was a slowing down of a hectic and confused life. For the first time I reflected on who I was and where my life was going. I spent a short period of feeling a little depressed as I adjusted to making my way about a totally new environment on crutches. In the midst of this inner questioning I discovered the spiritual side to my being and began to earnestly pray for the first time. In prayer I really encountered Christ. I began to read with a fresh imagination, and approach other people with a lighter heart. Social justice replaced pub-going as a primary in-terest. I gave DCU another go, after I had deferred the first year due to multiple operations on my ankle, only to last until Christmas. By then I had decided I wanted to study something with more depth and relevance to life – and the following September I began studying theology in St Patrick's College, Maynooth. It was a decision that raised a few eyebrows among my friends, not many of whom would have been sympathetic towards either religion or Catholicism. The three years there were ones of deepening friendships and appreciation for the intellectual foundations of my faith. They were punctuated by summers spent in Bogotá, working in an orphanage, and Rome, working in the Irish College. Needless to say, my undergraduate years were not monotonously idyllic – I sometimes became frustrated by doubt. But then sometimes faith and doubt are inseparable.

Thereafter, I completed a year of philosophy at University College Dublin. Though a wonderful academic experience, I never felt as 'at home' on the Belfield campus as I did in Maynooth, partly because I combined work with study and partly also because quite a lot of my attention was drawn towards my fiancée Caitríona – who is now my wife – and whom I first met while living in Maynooth. From UCD I was fortunate enough to fall into a job in politics, where I never imagined myself ending up, and was interested enough to continue studying – this time Human Rights Law in Trinity College, Dublin.

One of the key questions my burgeoning faith asked was the role of the Church in the life of a Catholic. I was well aware of the common critiques levelled at the Church by popular culture. It was only when I explored the intellectual foundations of these critiques, which I now know are centuries old, that I became confident enough to identify myself publicly as part of the Church. I came to realise that being a Catholic and being a member of the Catholic Church are inseparable – theologically, spiritually and practically. Over time I saw the co-dependency of Church and Catholicism as being necessitated by the fact that 'Catholic individualism' is a contradiction in terms. Individualism is too immature to admit the necessity of a living tradition for guidance, whereas the Church as the Body of Christ lives historically as a community of believers. The primary reason why the Church is rejected outside of atheism is not that believers reject her hypocrisy in favour of a purer relationship with God. Catholic teaching has never claimed that the Church is an elite club for the morally perfect, and yet this is the very presupposition of those who dispose themselves to denounce quickly, as distinct from criticise, the Church whenever failure occurs. The primary reason for the Church's rejection by believers is that the individual comes to the conclusion that they know Christ better than almost everyone else. I don't know Christ better than everyone else and I doubt such a thing is possible. Being part of the Church is for me to be inspired by the insights and teachings of a tradition that far transcend my limited horizons. It is to receive the grace of a living and active God who continues to walk with his pilgrim people and among all his children.

The Church today in Ireland is weaker than it has been for many generations, surely at least since before the event of Catholic emancipation. It is weaker in members, influence and maybe even theology. Yet weakness, which I do not mean in a wholly pejorative sense, is preferable to both impoverishment and legalism. In the past Irish Catholicism erred too much towards a narrow triumphalism. However, on occasions today it errs too much towards despair. There is an historical context to both tendencies, widely seen to be the rise and fall of Irish Catholicism. But this viewpoint interprets 'rise' and 'fall' through the lens of power and little else. The triumphalism evident in past Irish Catholicism mimicked to some extent that of imperialism in that success and quantifiable power were intertwined. For all its failings, liberalism offers a more exalted challenge to Catholicism than previous cultural paradigms. For the Irish Church to 'succeed' today she has to do so by her good works, faith, wisdom and charity. She can no longer rely on nationalism, superstition, bigotry, fear and implicit State sponsorship. This is not to endorse a simplistic and agenda-driven view of Irish history wherein the Church was the shackles on an innately poetic and romantic society. Instead, it is to argue against an illusion underpinning the despair of some sections of the Church:

that we are just exiting the Golden Age of Irish Catholicism. The Church gave Ireland not just the Gospel (its primary function) but also education, hope, identity and help in fostering a deep-rooted sense of both justice and compassion. Yet what she and her individual members have given they must continue to give. And as she has offended these values in the past she and her individual members must undertake not to offend again, otherwise our journey as a community of believers is hopelessly cyclical rather than joyously eschatological.

For all this the life of a Catholic is irreducible to ecclesiology. If a Catholic does not commit to love in a very personal capacity then no amount of communal observance will be enough to identify him/her as a true believer. This is real liberation – the freedom to love. Bound up with this commitment to love are all the personal dimensions to human life. Humility is involved – not just the humility to accept that I am oftentimes wrong, but also the humility to realise truth whenever and wherever it occurs, including the truth of revelation. Critical discernment is also involved due to the mutual dependency of faith and reason. This entails not scepticism, which as a form of egoism is closed to the truth, but reflexive criticism – the ability to critique not only one's faith and practices, but to critique the critiques also. There was little by way of reflexive criticism throughout a century scarred by the Catholic-orchestrated sexual abuse of vulnerable children in institutions and parishes. And there is little by way of reflexive criticism in a culture so quick to demonise paedophiles and yet so content both to sexualise young children and also to segregate sexuality from maturity and love. Neither rigorism nor liberalism knows the essence of human sexuality. There is a tendency among some believers to self-flagellate their Catholicism with newspaper editorials while blindly following some of the falsehoods championed by contemporary culture. Like any person of goodwill, I abhor how senior clergy violated the human rights of little children by ferrying paedophiles from parish to parish. But I don't uncritically accept that every voice condemning these atrocities speaks a coherent language of human rights in the first place. *In utero* child abuse still has many influential apologists.

Every thinking person lives life according to some set of doctrines, to some philosophy. What makes Catholicism so appealing to me on the philosophical level is its stress on the holistic interdependency of faith and reason, which translates also into the holistic interdependency of nature and grace. These doctrines taken together are the theological consequences of God becoming man and their practical implications are overwhelmingly life affirming. For one, they mean that it is natural for all of humankind to search freely for God, while natural also for God to love freely each and every human being without exception. They mean also that authentic faith is intrinsically reasonable while at the same time reason tends towards an affirmation of the divine. On the level of human existence these doctrines affirm the inseparability of body and soul – which has important consequences for how we understand mature human sexuality and interpersonal relationships in general. In terms of society, Catholic holism renders facile dualisms, whether political, religious or cultural, irrational. Hence the danger of too readily identifying the political dimensions of Catholicism with either the 'left' or the 'right'. These concepts are products of the political philosophy of the Enlightenment era and as such have limited applicability to a trans-historical religion. The same is true for the economic sphere; Catholic social teaching is neither socialism nor libertarianism but a juxtaposition of both. A further consequence of Catholic holism is the essential public dimension to the faith – a dimension which allows for genuine Catholic engagement with the realm of the political, what Aristotle understood as the maintaining of a just society.

All of this lacks meaning unless Christ is 'what it means to be a Catholic'. Not Christ in our image, as twenty-first century enlightened Europeans, but us in Christ's image so we may have fullness of life. Personally, I have a long way to go.

CHAPTER FIFTEEN

Standing Against Gravity

John Waters

Like a lot of public issues, religion is dogged by a short-circuiting language that communicates only what people already think, or think they think. Therefore, when you talk about God, it is necessary to reinvent language every time you open your mouth, and to blow up the spent words behind as you go. The subject as outlined – 'What being Catholic means to me' – threatens to draw us into this trap. If I sign up to it, my intervention will read as an assertion of membership of a club and imply that this membership is somehow pregnant with meaning, that the essence of my religiosity is my Catholicism and that this is something I desperately seek to defend.

For me this is entirely the wrong way round. Catholicism comes after the fact of my religiosity (an example of a word so mangled and distorted by the process I mentioned as to by now be capable of a startling resurrection). I am not religious because I am a Catholic, but Catholic because I am religious. My need for religion is like my need for air, and comes from approximately the same region of my body: my heart, nestling beside my lungs.

Religion has to do with my natural structure, my created-ness/creature-ness, my intrinsic desires, my dependence, my mortality, and my relationship with reality, pregnant with evidence of the Mystery that defines me. I call myself a Christian because for me this Mystery has at its centre the Presence of Christ, Lord of History. I am not an incidental phenomenon, randomly arrived and soon to depart, but an intrinsic part of infinite reality, my identity unbounded by the three-dimensional impediments or the laws and principles that govern this physical reality. That I am part of infinite time and space is a description of my very nature.

There is a hope inside me that is bigger than what the world thinks of as me, that overwhelms me with confidence and optimism and that rests its heavy expectation upon the light that it has placed just beyond my sight, beyond the horizon of human understanding. My desire tells me of the promise Christ made, a promise that something is always coming, something is always happening, something is always waiting for me just as I am always waiting for it. Nothing I can see, or hear or touch or smell comes near to satisfying this desire.

Catholicism comes into this because I was born a Catholic and, after years of running away, decided that the specificity of this cultural experience is vital to my sense of Christ, the Mystery Incarnate. Because there is this distance, this disproportionality, between what I hope for and what I can find in this dimension, I have in the past tended to shift around the place, mooching for a correspondence. Belatedly, it came to me: the optimal position resides in what is, in the specificity of what is there, which implicitly has been given for a reason. Our culture seduces us to think of what might be elsewhere, or different, or other. But the Other is already here, where we are, right now.

Our cultures do not understand what freedom is, defining it as the ability to do as you please, blind to man's experience which consistently reveals that this avenue of exploration leads to disgust and disaster. Real freedom resides beyond our reach, like a shape floating in the corner of the eye. Only in repose do we begin to see its shape.

For all kinds of reasons to do with corrupted notions of both religion and freedom, our cultures have been led to believe that religiosity is something imposed, and therefore something that can be discarded at will, in order to be more 'free'. This is an impossibility, because religion is an original essence of the human being. You can, of course, claim you have 'moved beyond it', as I did for nearly twenty years, but this won't change your fundamental structure. Religion is not a choice, but a fact. We may choose to identify ourselves outside the embrace of formal religion, but this changes nothing. Our natures remain.

Our culture, having no sense of what freedom is, inculcates a tendency to seek everything except what is there, and therefore leads us to think that we can achieve freedom by becoming other than we are. But there is no need to be anywhere else. Where I am now is absolute and unchangeable.

I am not a Hindu. I am not Buddhist. If you have a path, why waste time looking for one? I see no point in fighting the Catholic Church any more than I might think it a good idea to fight the air or kick a tree. Neither do I see the Church as a refuge or a club, or a political party, still less a source of moral guidance. The Church is where I look in order to maintain a structured engagement with the Mystery, and also in my need for a source of reflective experience of the human condition.

The Catholic Church, including the Irish Church, has many political and even ideological manifestations, but I have no more that a journalist's or a magpie's interest in these. Belonging to the Church doesn't for me relate to any social or political circumstance, but to my fundamental humanity and destiny, to my relationship with reality and with Infinity, which is just another word for Mystery. This, not Catholicism, is my religious identity.

There is, too, a deadly virus in our culture which separates believing from knowing, the idea that religion comprises the action of going into some room, even a very big room, getting on your knees and scrunching up your brain in an attempt to 'believe' something, and then entering a hostile world holding this quality of 'faith' in front like a shield. This is nonsense. Faith is not an irrational leap in the dark, but the reasonable response to the real.

Reality is God-given. It therefore cannot be hostile to God, except in a superficial manmade way. Man's inability to accept the limits of his own structure has created conditions of thought in our cultures which are hostile to the idea of a God, but reality itself is neither hostile nor neutral towards someone seeking to connect with the infinite dimension of being.

'Belief' doesn't come into it. Faith is knowledge, which derives from experience of the promise with which reality is pregnant. I cannot 'believe' in God by looking at reality – I can only know that he is. This is a reasonable inference – the only reasonable one - from reality and my experience of it. Religion involves not some esoteric engagement with the mystical, but the prosaic process of going into the great outdoors knowing what I am engaged in and open to seeing what is there. Reality cannot, by definition, be other than sympathetic to my essential condition, which is religious. Faith, then, is the force that animates my total humanity, that allows me to stand up straight against gravity and wait in hope for what is promised.

Either God made the world or he did not make the world. There are no other possibilities. If I decide to maintain that he did not make the world, I have to come up with a better explanation, and this has for millennia taxed more dedicated minds than mine. I need, just to exist, a working hypothesis of reality in its totality, and only the God hypothesis gives me that. Without the concept of God, then, I am disconnected from reality, from my infinite circuitry, and am, by definition, unfree.

If I know, which I do, that there is more to reality than what I see hear and touch, I need some affirmation, some structural entity that will make that relationship real and in the culture that I'm in, this means the Christian proposal. The Christian event is not a story, not history, not a morality tale, but an Event of this very moment. The resurrection happens moment to moment before our eyes, but in our pessimism we look and see nothing but randomness. Christianity cannot really be transmitted by theologians, only by witnesses who see clearly and describe what is there.

This is where Catholicism figures in my life. It is where I go to be educated about my deeper structure and nature, and where I find companionship for the journey towards my destination. The Church fails me most of the time, as I fail myself most of the time, but without it I might be alone in a culture that denies my nature at every turn. The trouble is: if I am disposed to place my faith in the Great Hope, then the shopkeepers and the prostitutes have a problem selling me things that may momentarily strike me as the answer to the question my humanity exudes.

Most people cannot even approach this fundamental truth about themselves because the initial access from our culture needs to be achieved through language, which has been booby-trapped by a ideological war waged on the one hand by a faction too 'modern' and 'intelligent' to give any credence to the idea that that man is fundamentally religious, and on the other by those calling themselves religious-minded, who have fuelled what is called secularism by holding faith up as a moral shield against the world. Between these two warring sides we must find the true essence of our humanity.

Faith is no more than honesty before reality. What do I see? Where did it come from? And then, where did I come from? What or who made me? What makes me now, in this moment, if I do not make myself? Sooner or later, the true intelligence arrives at God, because God is what intelligence derives from.

The Fullness of Life

D. Vincent Twomey SVD

What being a Catholic means to me is, very simply, the fullness of life. Jesus promised the faithful, 'I came that they may have life and have it in fullness' (John 10:10). This is precisely what is made possible by being a Catholic, provided we respond with generosity to what the Church offers us. The earliest use of the Greek term from which we derive the English word 'Catholic' is found c. AD 107 in the writings of St Ignatius of Antioch (Sm 8,2). It originally meant universal or all embracing. More specifically, the term Catholic refers to the universality of the Christian truth and love that knows no bounds, that cuts across all borders, be they political, social, economic or otherwise, and thus constitutes the Church as One.

Today in Ireland the term Catholic has a sectarian ring about it, which is usually exacerbated by the predicate 'Roman'. There are various causes for this undermining of the original meaning. For example, in the nineteenth century, the Catholic Church was but one of a number of non-conformist Christian denominations in a state – the United Kingdom of Great Britain and Ireland – which recognised the Anglican Communion as the Established Church. To distinguish it from the Anglican Communion, which also claims to be catholic, a claim made plausible by the spread of Anglicans throughout the British Empire, the term Roman Catholic was preferred, thus implying in turn a kind of local church (Italian, as it were). This, in turn, obfuscates the real significance of the adjective 'Roman', which originally meant communion of the bishop of the local church (diocese) with the Bishop of Rome, the Successor to St Peter, Chief of the Apostles, the visible sign of the invisible unity or universality of the

Church. 'Roman', strange to say, also means universal – the universal communion of local churches.

The 'Troubles' in the North, usually depicted in the media as Catholic versus Protestant, even for those who should know better in the Republic, helped confirm the 'sectarian' ring to the term 'Catholic', especially for those who championed a 'modern, secular Ireland' in the shadow of the civil strife raging in the North.

But even before the recent civil strife broke out in the North, critically-minded Catholics in the Republic, such as Seán Ó Faoláin, questioned the credentials of the Irish Church to be truly Catholic. The identity of Catholicism and nationalism for political purposes in the nineteenth century, and the apotheosis of this in the Irish Free State in the first half of the twentieth century, contributed to the undermining of her true catholic nature. The Irish Church became almost exclusively a local or national church, albeit with a diaspora abroad where Catholic émigrés were often even more nationalist than those who stayed at home. One must also mention the narrow-mindedness of so-called 'traditional Irish Catholicism' that was steeped in a mixture of Victorian Puritanism and a type of Catholic moral theology that was legalistic and primarily concerned with sin.

There were, of course, more positive counter-forces that helped retain essential aspects of true catholicity, namely the stress on the universal mercy and forgiveness of God as fostered by devotion to the Sacred Heart, the recognition of the Pope as head of the Church on earth, and the so-called 'foreign missions' of the late-nineteenth and early-twentieth century that made Irish Catholics conscious of the world Church, at least to a certain degree. So too, the Irish love of sport and play – helped significantly by the GAA – prevented some of the more negative effects of Protestant influence, such as Sabbatarianism, from taking hold. Celebration is central to the fullness of life that is Catholicism.

I discovered the true richness of Catholicism first in my studies for the priesthood in the Divine Word Seminary in Donamon where I was introduced to the questioning nature of philosophy and the richness of Catholic theology and liturgy. It was the time of the Second Vatican Council, which recovered much of that true Catholicity which, even in countries richer in a Catholic cultural tradition than Ireland, had been endangered by the post-Tridentine effort to overcome the challenge of the Reformation. I still remember the excitement of discovering the inexhaustible source of inspiration that is scripture, Old and New Testaments, as well as the different moods of the liturgical year, such as melancholy of Advent with its longing for the coming of 'the desired of the Nations', a mood which the Irish Church has yet to discover. I recall the first lectures I attended in theology, when our Novice Master, Father Brendan O'Reilly SVD, initiated us day-by-day into the mysteries of the faith. It was truly awe-inspiring. In our final year in Donamon, we were presented with the first English translation of the documents of Vatican II (by Father Austin Flannery OP). We devoured them.

By comparison, Maynooth was a great disappointment. Theology in Maynooth is best passed over in silence, apart from recognising a few exceptional lecturers, Donal Flanagan in dogma, Enda McDonagh in fundamental moral theology, and, especially, Patrick J. Corish in Church history. It was in Germany that I discovered the excitement of theology as an academic discipline that stretches the intellect as much as it can touch the heart, when properly taught. Admittedly, not all lecturers in Germany did that; some had succumbed to one or other of the perennial temptations of academic theology, namely preoccupation with the formalities of scholarship as an academic discipline or the emptying of theology into an ideology (either liberal or conservative). In both cases, what is avoided is the hard search for truth that involves no little self-criticism, including an examination of one's own theological and philosophical assumptions. When I went to Regensburg for postgraduate study under the direction of the then Professor Joseph Ratzinger, I was fully initiated, as it were, into that search for truth and the intellectual stimulation it engenders. His lectures, seminars and doctoral colloquium were models of theology at its most rigorous and at its most exciting. He was not alone. The faculty as a whole was an exciting one, where most of the diverse strains of Catholic theology of the time were represented by one or other professor.

In Germany, I also came into extended contact with a Catholic cultural tradition that, unlike the Irish cultural tradition, was largely unbroken since the Middle Ages (and sometimes older, since many local churches, like Cologne and Trier, trace their Christian origin to the third century, if not earlier). While I was at Regensburg, the Cathedral Choir (*die Domspatzen*, cathedral sparrows, as they are affectionately known locally) celebrated the thousandth anniversary of its foundation. It enjoys an unbroken tradition. Incidentally, the choir-master, also director of the Cathedral Choir boarding school, was Georg Ratzinger, the brother of the present Pope. The city has a vast number of churches of every architectural style and epoch, some reaching back to the third century and mostly still in use for worship: Romanesque, Gothic, Baroque, Rococo, neo-classical, neo-Gothic and ultra modern.

My favourite church is the Schottenkirche, the twelfth-century Romanesque church of St James' Abbey in Regensburg, which is now the diocesan seminary. It was originally the monastery church of the Irish Benedictine monks who came originally from priories in Rosscarbery and Cashel. They were the last of the Irish missionaries to continental Europe who helped fashion European civilisation. The architect of Cormac's chapel on the Rock of Cashel was probably a monk of that ancient monastery. According to Canon Thomas Finan, the inspiration for Dante's *Divine Comedy* was provided by the poem of an Irish monk of the Abbey, which recalled the experience of St Patrick's Purgatory. I said Mass daily in that magnificent abbey church, under whose altar are kept the relics of Blessed Muiredach (or Mercherdach), the hermit-founder of the original monastery. And it was there that Professor Ratzinger held his fortnightly doctoral colloquium. The scallop shell, symbol of pilgrims to St James in Compostella, now in his papal coat of arms, was taken from the coat of arms of former abbots.

But it was in Germany, Austria, Switzerland, France, Poland, and Italy that I also experienced something more indicative of the richness of the European cultural tradition that was inspired by the Catholic faith: the saints and art. Ratzinger once said that the most convincing *apologia* for the truth of the faith was to be found in both the lives of the saints and the magnificent art and music inspired by that same faith. Evidence of both abounds all over Europe. The works of art are not just museum pieces and the great achievements of church music are not limited to concert performances. The saints continue to be celebrated in festive mood in the architectural masterpieces they inspired and with the music composed by musicians such as Palestrina, Haydn, Mozart, Fauré, and Bruckner. Catholic Europe knows how to celebrate.

Teaching in the Regional Seminary of the Holy Spirit, Bomana, Papua New Guinea, enabled me once again not only to appreciate the original meaning of Catholic, namely the universality of the truth, but also its perennial youthfulness. Despite enormous difficulties, the faith had, within a little over a century, taken root in the hearts and minds of these people who had preserved their tribal traditions for tens of thousands of years, traditions that are precious witnesses to the primordial cultures of mankind. Like all religious-cultural traditions, these too found their fulfilment in the Catholic faith. There I taught the theological tract on sacraments and so had occasion to study, however inadequately, the rituals of these and similar aboriginal peoples, as well as look at their place in comparative religious studies. It was then that I discovered the cultural and existential roots of the Catholic sacramental system. The key to this discovery was provided by two essays on the theology of the sacraments by Joseph Ratzinger. When I returned to Europe, I presented my discoveries when teaching at the SVD Theology Faculty near Vienna and later, as Visiting Professor in Fribourg, Switzerland. But what my short time in Papua New Guinea taught me above all was the way truth and love crosses all barriers, cultural, historical, social or economic, and how the Holy Spirit through the instrumentality of weak, human missionaries from Europe, American and Australia, touched the hearts of these people. This young church has had one of its own raised to the honours of the altar: the catechist Blessed Peter de Rot.

My experience of the true catholicity of the Church and its youthfulness was deepened during a visit to the Church in China as a member of an (unofficial) delegation from the Irish Church organised by a subcommittee of the Irish Missionary Union. It was led with panache by Bishop Willie Walsh. The vigour of a faith that had survived decades of severe persecution as an underground church was palpable. In China, it is above all the intellectuals who are turning to Christianity in droves, since their own cultural traditions had evidently failed to halt the devastation of modernity (expressed most dramatically in that form of radical Marxism known as Maoism). What happened in the early Church is happening again. One of the greatest Chinese thinkers of the twentieth century, John Wu, once compared the wisdom of the great Chinese philosophers to pure crystal water that had been transformed into wine in the writings of what he considered the greatest psychologist of the modern world, St Thérèse of Lisieux. That also sums up the relationship between the wisdom traditions of the world religions and the Catholic faith.

At a more personal level, I am grateful to God for ensuring that the truth revealed in Christ has been handed on in integral form from the time of the apostles down to our own day – thanks to the work of the Holy Spirit and despite the all-too-evident human weakness of the successors of the apostles, including several popes. The essence of that teaching is be found brilliantly presented in the new *Catechism of the Catholic Church*, a unique achievement that only the Catholic Church could produce – an achievement yet to be 'received' at the local level in Ireland. How thankful am I for the gift of the papacy, the divinely-given guarantee of Christ's truth – most recently manifested in the encyclicals of the recent popes on social and moral issues, not least of which is that of Paul VI, *Humanae Vitae*, despite the massive rejection of same by the modern world. The Church also provides the healing needed by those whose conscience has been touched by the Church's teaching and who seek reconciliation and the mercy of God. I am grateful to God for the fullness of the sacramental system that is found in the Catholic Church, at the centre of which is the Holy Eucharist, the real presence that transforms the world from within. I rejoice in the Church's teaching regarding the effectiveness of the sacraments, irrespective of the moral quality of those who administer them, in particular the sacrament of penance. As a priest only too conscious of his own failings, this is a particular joy and comfort.

Penance and joy, human suffering and divine hope, immediately bring to mind Lourdes and the various Marian shrines around the world which the Church has approved after serious study and which are but variations of the same themes: Guadalupe, Knock, Fatima, etc. One should also mention the countless Marian shrines in Europe that owe their origin not to any heavenly apparition but to the deeply ingrained love Catholics have for the Mother of their Lord and Saviour and who seek her intercession in times of trial. Their mundane devotion enabled the shines of Altötting in Bavaria and Montserrat in Spain to survive the centuries. With regard to prayer, being Catholic embraces the most diverse forms of prayer and devotions – from the simple Rosary to the mystical heights of a St John of the Cross or a St Teresa of Avila.

And as a student of moral theology, I rejoice at the way the Catholic Church has been able to recover in the last decade or so the moral vision that inspired the great teachers of the Church from St Basil and St Augustine to St Thomas Aquinas, but which, to a great extent, tended to get lost after Trent, though never entirely, as the example of St Alphonsus Liguori teaches us. That moral vision, rooted in the human and divine virtues, is presented in the new *Catechism* as a means to the end of human fulfilment and ultimate happiness. But, as Pope Benedict XVI has pointed out, the Church's moral teaching is secondary to the primacy of friendship with Jesus Christ, true God and true Man.

In other words, the Pope wants to stress the primacy of grace. And it is that friendship with Christ which the entire edifice of the Catholic Church serves, thanks to the Holy Spirit working in and through it, as its ultimate goal. The fact that other, less inspiring goals have, over the centuries, time and again impinged on the daily life of the Church does not take away from the more important fact that God in Christ through the Holy Spirit continues to break through human weakness. All of this can be experienced at times in the Divine Liturgy when celebrated as the Church intends – when mind and heart and all the human senses are touched and we are interiorly transformed in worship of the Trice Holy God.

Catholicism: Finding Personal Meaning

Patricia Casey

I clearly recall that day in May when I made my Confirmation. In those days girls still wore white dresses and veils, although be-suited ones were just beginning to make an appearance. Of course, within five years dresses and veils had vanished and are now only remembered as spectacles from quaint and more innocent times. That morning, as I walked up the aisle and the moment approached when the bishop was anointing my forehead with chrism and sealing my fate as a 'strong and perfect Christian and soldier of Jesus Christ,' I reflected on what this might mean for my future. Proceeding along what seemed an interminably long aisle, I recognised that I had no choice in whether I should receive Confirmation or not – after all, I couldn't very well refuse the bishop's call, as the disgrace to my family and to my reputation throughout the diocese would draw the sternest opprobrium. I recall the moment of realisation that what mattered was not what I said in response to the incantation but what my heart told me. And on that day it told me that I should try to stand by a faith that, even then, I recognised as having already had a central role in shaping my personality.

Since that morning of blissful innocence my faith has been tested many times and even to this day some of my questions are without complete resolution. Does God exist? If he does, what is his purpose? Why does he allow suffering, particularly of children? What of those who are not comforted by their faith in times of trouble? Attempts to resolve my uncertainty about the purpose of suffering have been unsatisfactory. I have always considered the usual response, that God is mysterious and doesn't show us his true purpose, to be a disguise for incomprehension. The analogy of the will of God as resembling a tapestry with its clear pattern on one side and a mish-mash of untidy threads of the other is for me a simile that has no real personal resonance. The truth, I believe, is that there is no answer to these questions and in particular to those relating to suffering.

Yet for all my doubts and questions, there is a very powerful religious impulse that has led humankind to engage routinely in religious rituals and to turn to God for solace at times of difficulty; this same urge has spawned millions of converts through the ages, to all faiths and to Catholicism in particular, and has led people to return to their faith after decades of neglect or even hostility. And although I feel as did St Thomas, the doubter, that I would wish God to make himself more visible to us, especially when we most need him, the religious drive remains remarkably powerful and I continue to be drawn to this faith, both intellectually and emotionally.

Corruption by power

I have chosen to remain a member of the Catholic Church notwithstanding the knowledge that it is imperfect. But I will not be an apologist for these grave matters – for the Church, most notably in Ireland, the United States and Australia, which treated vulnerable children with indescribable cruelty and depravity and then provided the abusers with sanctuary. I recognise that these abuses have alienated many and that I may appear to be ignoring the suffering of those who were entrusted to the love of the servants of Jesus on earth, yet were the victims of abuse by these same people. Yet I am aware that institutions have always engaged in abuse, be it sexual, physical or financial, when they held positions of power in society. Indeed governments, past and present, throughout the world, continue to facilitate the abuse of the vulnerable by the powerful in its various guises – men had authority over women until female emancipation, slaves were treated as less than human by the owners, black people were segregated and regarded as non-persons until recently in South Africa, unborn children are killed in large numbers in the name of freedom of choice and governments legislate for the killing of those found guilty of certain crimes in some countries still. So the problem of abuse of the vulnerable by the powerful is not specific to the Catholic Church – the problem of abuse exists wherever humans and institutions are in positions of power over others. If only the transgressors and their facilitators in the Catholic Church had followed the teachings of Jesus to 'love one another as I have loved you' and paid heed to his words, 'But if anyone causes one of these little ones who believe in me to sin, it would be better for him to have a large millstone hung around his neck and to be drowned in the depths of the sea' (Matthew 18:6).

Why am I still a Catholic?
Religious sociologists speak of several dimensions to faith as follows:

the doctrinal (the beliefs of the particular religion);

the intellectual (knowledge about one's religion);

the ethical-consequential (behaviour influenced by Church teachings);

the ritualistic (religious practices, later divided into private activities and public rituals);

the experiential (feelings of closeness to God);

the social (being part of a community).

These will be present to varying extents in all of those professing a faith. For me the most relevant are the ethical-consequential, the ritualistic and the social. Of course, these are not mutually exclusive and clearly they interconnect.

My Catholic faith has led me to the firm conviction that we all need structure and boundaries within which we can exercise our autonomy. Unfettered autonomy only results in selfishness and anarchy. For me, Catholicism provides this guidance on how we should conduct our lives. Some might argue that it is a sign of immaturity or of some other deficiency to have to rely on institutions to promote and reinforce our good behaviour. However, this is a universal requirement – hence the need for civil laws to curb unacceptable behaviours. And this for me is one potent reason for remaining a Catholic. The teaching of my Church provides an ethical framework around which I can attempt to live my life. Right and wrong are clearly enunciated and there is a mechanism, contained in a ritual, through which I can attempt to address my wrongdoings.

As a psychiatrist I see parallels between the boundaries set by mental health professionals and the injunctions laid down by the churches. Indeed the absence of boundaries can have serious consequences for individuals themselves, for those with whom they have relationships and for society as a whole. Thus, I cannot object to a religion proscribing certain behaviours when I, as a mental health professional, do the same; only the target and methods used differ, not the principle.

Guilt – good and bad
There is a belief that the Catholic Church in particular creates a guilt-ridden people because of its preoccupation with sin, especially those of a sexual nature. But my faith has also taught me that emotions such as guilt are at times appropriate and are not necessarily pathological. Indeed guilt is a good teacher since it allows us to discern what is right and what is wrong at any time. Guilt is only pathological when it accrues from pecadillos or when it endures after suitable reparation has been made.

Within Catholicism wrongdoings can be expiated and guilt assuaged by the sacrament of Confession. Of course, those of all faiths and of none will have a mechanism by which forgiveness can occur. People of other faiths will argue, quite rightly, that sorrow comes from the heart and that no human, not even a priest, has the power to forgive sin except God; and that sorrow for sin comes from within rather than from any external source such as a priest in confession. None of these perspectives is incorrect and all are true of those receiving the sacrament of Confession also. Yet confession allows us to externalise our sorrow by having to speak the sin to another. Admitting our faults and weaknesses is for many psychologically taboo and requires motivation and insight. Being a Catholic, for me, means that I have to overcome my instinctive avoidance of confronting my flaws by admitting them to myself and then taking the further step of making them explicit to another. The process and ritual of confession, culminating in forgiveness and a 'firm purpose of amendment', is a religious tool that has enormous therapeutic potential, which I am privileged to have at my disposal.

'You don't need religion to be happy or good'
When one speaks of the benefits of religious belief and practice the reply is often that surely happiness and virtue aren't just the prerogative of people of faith. Those who are atheists or simply doubtful can be equally contented and moral and have as much meaning in their lives as those who are devout in their chosen faith. Along similar lines there is also the statement that being 'spiritual' is as valuable as being religious and that denomin-ational affiliation is irrelevant. But the term 'spirituality' has a broad compass that ranges from accepting 'Gaia' as a living entity to believing that life has meaning. Spiritual experiences might include crystal gazing or meditation or neither. No rules or in-junctions are imposed, apart from striving to do good. Deciding what is right and what wrong is a decision made only from within the person since spirituality does not have its own 'Bible' equivalent. Specific tenets do not exist and values are largely determined internally rather than by external considerations. Expressed in common parlance it runs, 'If you feel it is right for you, then it's OK.' Of course, some would contend that religious hermits are equally inward-looking but this is an inaccurate per-ception since their perspective is not to achieve self-fulfilment but towards achieving the wellbeing of others and the world at large, directed by an ethical framework that is not based on cur-rent emotional needs but on a tradition that has been established over millennia. Spirituality could be described as religion for an atomised age that accepts any pre-determined core truths.

Numerous studies now point to the social and psychological benefits of the practice of religion and these extend to areas such as crime, suicide, depression, marital harmony, teenage impulsivity and a host of others. So this confounds the received wisdom concerning the egalitarianism of religion as against spirituality. It seems that there is something definite attaching to the rituals of religious practice. And when it comes to unpacking the benefits of religious practice as compared to spirituality, there is strong evidence of the benefits of both compared to having no religious beliefs, but there is now an emerging body of science identifying institutional religious practice as the richest source of psycho-social strength. This has been examined specifically with respect to protection against suicide and against mental illness. This does not mean that religious people have a complete armour against these, but it shows that on average those who are religious are less likely to develop these conditions, and if they do then their severity is less when compared to those who describe themselves as spiritual or who have no particular beliefs. So although belief in God and adherence to a particular faith may be a personal matter, it has ramifications beyond the personal. For me it is heartening that my inclinations have a scientific backing.

'All religions are the same'

But why choose Catholicism? It has become fashionable to claim that 'all religions are the same' and that particular denominational affiliation is irrelevant. For me the distinctions have always mattered and this has stemmed from my strongly held democratic beliefs and roots. I have never understood the popular leanings of ecumenism. This is not to say that other faiths should not be respected; indeed they represent for me a validation of the value of difference. Surely we should accept that specific faiths and the differences they represent have stemmed from the different perspectives of their founders and adherents. To blur these distinctions is a bland attempt at denying the reality of difference. Why should churches want all their members to have similar understandings of their precepts and demand that they express their beliefs similarly?

The unbroken historical link between the Pope and St Peter is a reminder that I am a member of the Church founded by Jesus. The overseeing role of the popes, the successors to St Peter, in moulding the precepts of the early Christians into a rich theology that has current relevance while being firmly rooted on the teachings of Christ has prevented Catholicism from ossifying.

The community of believers

One aspect of my religious practice that I value especially is being part of a community of believers. Of course, the most obvious element is experiencing the friendship of one's own parish and their support at times of sorrow, especially bereavement, or celebrations such as weddings.

However, besides friendship and support, it is also reassuring to know that there are many others in one's community who share similar principles and who draw from the same wellspring of teaching and of spirituality. And this is even more obvious when worshipping abroad, be it Chicago or Bombay, London or Oslo. The feeling of being part of a large and global movement and not just a loner in personal communication with God is reassuring and comforting. John Donne was aware of this when he wrote, 'No man is an island entire of itself; every man is a piece of the continent, a part of the main.'

Irritations

Being a Catholic also has its irritations. The liberal media and public often seek to define one's position on various issues by looking to one's religion. For example, it is often assumed that one's religion is the only determining influence on views relating to the benefits of marriage, while the possibility that this position might be supported by science is conveniently ignored. Such one-dimensional thinking is, in my opinion, based on the belief that the critical faculties of Catholics are in a strait jacket, as if our intellect is fossilised and incapable of logical thought.

On the other side of the coin, I am very aware that being a Catholic means that I am a member of a church organisation which, in Ireland at any rate, is poor at communicating and even poorer at rectifying errors it has made in the past, such as those relating to the sexual abuse of children. Having been damaged by the activities of those who should have been protecting children, the Church in Ireland has often reinforced negative stereotypes by its defensive and awkward approach to such matters. On other matters, the Church is often slow in responding to pressing matters of public concern and while it is accepted that it thinks in centuries rather than in days, this reticence can be at best frustrating and at worst detrimental.

Attack – the ultimate compliment

Visiting the Vatican, the centre of the Catholic Church, it is difficult to comprehend that it is from here that the spiritual welfare of some two billion people is directed. There seems a contradiction between the minuteness of Vatican City and the huge membership it claims. Contemplating the venom often directed at various Church documents and pronouncements and at the man who personifies the Church, that is, the Pope, it seems remarkable that such a small geographic area and so old a man could generate such ire. For many, the constant attacks on the Church and its teachings are a source of sadness and regret, but for me they are the opposite. I see it as a compliment that its global influence is recognised to the extent that it draws such significant criticism from those who disagree with its teachings. After all, silence is the mask of indifference.

Being a Catholic is as much part of me as being a woman or being Irish. It suffused my being at a formative period and it continues to guide my life. It protects me from my own weaknesses and failings. When I worship I feel enriched, when I confess I feel renewed. I know that I am a member of a faith with historical links to Jesus himself and that I am part of something greater than the two billion individuals who make up the faith. The all-encompassing nature of Catholicism is awesome, like a mother's love for her children.

This, and more, is what being a Catholic means to me.

Catholic in a Culture of Choice

Andrew O'Connell

The big questions

We were not aware of it at the time but my grandmother was in the final weeks of her life. I was a student in University College Cork and, in true student fashion, I availed of the weekend opportunities to return home to Kerry to avail of the home comforts. On Sunday nights I would take the late bus back to Cork and would call to say goodbye to her.

She was the real Irish grandmother with a great devotional faith and an unshakeable belief in the power of holy water. As children we would be just about to fall asleep at night time when the bedroom door would open and we would be drowned in our beds with a liberal shower of holy water.

On this particular Sunday evening I called to say goodnight. I had a key for her front door and I went to the kitchen where she was usually to be found. Curiously there was no sound in the house – no radio, no television. When I opened the kitchen door I found her stretched out on the sofa. Thinking that she was asleep and knowing that, God rest her, she wouldn't thank you for waking her during a nap, I turned to leave. Just at that moment I saw a little bit of movement by her side. She wasn't entirely asleep, she was probably dozing and she was praying the Rosary.

I left her to it and walked back home.

On the bus back to Cork that evening the image of my grandmother and the rosary beads pushed me to wonder what it would be that my generation would have in our hands when we would be lying flat on our backs staring at the white ceiling in the final days of our lives. My suspicion is that a lot of what we surround ourselves with today – iPods, mobile phones, internet, all marvellous in themselves – will be of little assistance to us when we come to face the big, big questions of life. Questions such as where did we come from, why are we here, and what will happen after we take our final breath?

Sadly, the decline in faith in Ireland over recent years has been accompanied by a decline in an interest in engaging with these big questions of life.

Some might dismiss the faith of my grandparents' generation as simple piety suited to a different Ireland of rural, superstitious, poorly educated people. But what I saw was a woman facing into her final days with a faith that provided meaning to her existence and which helped her to make sense of her life, her last days and all that was to come after.

And so to answer directly the theme of this book, 'What being Catholic means to me?'

It means meaning.

A big answer

Socrates, rather dismissively, felt that 'an unexamined life is not worth living.' I can honestly say that it is faith which has prompted me to examine life and it is only through the lens of faith that I can see a reason for my life.

However, Catholicism is not simply an invitation to endless questioning and wondering. Catholicism also offers a great proposal, a great answer – a God who is love.

In the postmodern world in which we live there is the very real risk that individuals come to see themselves as infinitesimally small and meaningless specks on a vast cosmos of space and time. It is tempting to conclude that one's life is just a minor event in some astrophysical phenomenon which we do not fully understand.

Catholicism challenges this bleak conclusion, a conclusion which leads to loneliness and despair. Instead, Catholicism proposes that we have been loved into existence by God who has counted every hair on our head.

Pope Benedict XVI put it beautifully in his homily at the Easter Vigil in 2008 when he said: 'Yes, I believe that the world and my life are not the product of chance, but the product of eternal reason and eternal love. They are created by Almighty God.'

So, what do I believe? I believe that I am not just an accident of circumstances. I believe that I was loved into being by God who is love. The cynic will argue that this is merely a device employed by all generations of human beings in order to make sense of their existence because we simply cannot face the reality that we are merely an astrophysical accident. They will point out that Christianity is merely one in a long line of myths which people have relied on to rationalise their existence.

They will claim that there are a number of ancient myths which also involve a son of a god-like figure who is killed and comes back to life again. For instance, Dionysus, the son of Zeus, king of the gods, is killed by his followers only to be revived again by his father, Zeus.

While this might shake the faith of some, it is precisely this which made the faith of C. S. Lewis, who saw the telling of these myths as a great yearning, a longing, among those ancient peoples for that story to be real, to happen, to be fact.

In Christianity, Lewis concluded that myth has become fact. A man called Jesus existed. Eyewitnesses tell us that he rose from the dead. We can choose to believe or not to believe but there is no question but this man did exist. In Jesus, God has answered the deepest longing of people.

Communicating faith

Very often I am invited to speak to gatherings in schools, in staff rooms and in parishes. Frequently, at the end of the presentation I am approached by a mother who tells me that she has a son my age and she can't get him inside the door of the church. 'What should I say to him?' she asks. I have no formula of words to offer which will guarantee success. Even though this is the age of instant communication, there are no instant missionary tactics.

What I can say, however, is that it was the power of example of my grandmother's faith that put me on the road to curiosity and which led me to make a commitment to my own faith. Perhaps that is the best way for that woman to engage with her son – through the power of her example, by being as joyful and as genuine a witness to the faith as she can be.

These are very difficult times for those of an older generation who feel they lack the language to communicate to a younger generation what it is that their faith, the faith that they love, means to them.

This is not a surprise. We are living through a revolution. Many years from now it will appear in the history books as *the communications revolution* or *the technological revolution* alongside other epochs in history such as the *French* and *Industrial revolutions*.

The significance of this is that the instant communication culture of Bebo, Facebook and the ubiquitous mobile phone has also created what could be termed a culture of distraction.

All of these technological distractions have helped construct a cocoon around us, allowing us to live quite happily without ever engaging with the really meaningful questions of life. Perhaps one of the greatest tasks of the Church today is to tap on that cocoon and to remind people that there are some big issues to engage with.

Interestingly, the author Colm Tóibín, who is by no means an apologist for Catholicism, recently offered advice to the Church. He said that the Church should reclaim Sunday. He admitted that, in the past, Sunday was a day of boredom but at least it offered the possibility and opportunity for introspection.

The promise that the age of technology would herald a leisure culture has failed spectacularly. The recent news that we will soon be able to use mobile phones and the internet on flights was not hailed as another wonderful technological advance, especially among young professionals who often enjoy flying as it is the only period when they know they will not be bothered. It is remarkable to think that some people now feel that the only place to find some peace and quiet is 35,000 feet above the earth.

The theologian Karl Rahner predicted that 'the Christian of the future will be a mystic or will not exist at all.' What precisely this mysticism will look like is unclear but it will almost certainly involve introspection, reflection and an examination of the world and of life, something which is not encouraged by the prevailing culture.

At the current pace anyone who chooses not to listen to an iPod when they go for a long walk will earn the label mystic.

Why bother?

The title of this book is 'What being Catholic means to me.' While I have answered that question with 'quite a lot', many of my friends answer 'not a whole lot'.

Believing today demands a conscious decision. We are Catholics in a culture of choice. This is a very different experience from being a cradle or a cultural Catholic.

The former Master of the Dominican Order and author, Timothy Radcliffe OP, tells the story of how he worked in an office in London before becoming a priest. There for the first time he met non-Catholics who asked him questions about his beliefs. After a period of being quizzed about his faith, he came to the conclusion that if he was really to practise his faith then 'it must be the most important thing in my life. If it is not then perhaps I should just give it up.'

This was almost identical to my own experience. I could not believe that God took human flesh, lived among us, died for us and rose from the dead, and confine that to the occasional thirty minute Service on a Sunday morning. It must mean more.

C. S. Lewis knew this too when he wrote in *God in the Dock*:

Christianity, if false, is of no importance.
Christianity, if true, is of infinite importance.
Christianity can never be of moderate importance.

For me, *no importance* translated to *not practising at all*. Moderate importance was going to be the occasional thirty minute Service on a Sunday. And to be honest I am still trying to work out what it means to make my faith something of infinite importance in my life

When asked the question 'Why bother believing?', many believers will answer with the word *hope*. In my experience of working with groups, it often takes a lot of discussion before believers can identify the precise nature of that hope. St Augustine was quite clear about it: '*Resurrectio Domini spes nostra* – the Lord's resurrection is our hope.'

I think we saw a beautiful example of this in the midst of the media circus which was the death of Jade Goody, the late Big Brother contestant in the United Kingdom. Jade asked to be baptised when she discovered that she was ill. She also asked that her two young sons be baptised. In what was surely grace at work, she said sorry and asked forgiveness from those she had hurt and offended during her life. It was the hope of the resurrection that enabled a twenty-seven-year-old terminally ill mother to look at her sons and, with a broken heart but a smile on her face, tell them that she was going to look after them and pray for them from heaven when she was no longer among them. That is the hope that our faith offers.

Those who propose that religious cultures of faith can be replaced with a faith-neutral culture of value ethics don't seem to realise that it is only faith that can offer a hope as powerful as that seen in the final days of that woman's life.

Back to the beginning
One of the nicest places to spend a Sunday afternoon in Dublin is the site of the Fifteen Acres in the Phoenix Park.

The Fifteen Acres is in fact about two hundred acres in size and at one end of the park stands the papal cross which marks the spot where Pope John Paul II celebrated Mass on the first day of his 1979 visit, an event which has now assumed the aura of a legend.

At the foot of the cross is a marble slab onto which is engraved just one line from the Pope's homily from that day. It reads: 'Be converted every day.' For me this is the challenge of my faith. Catholicism means a daily drama of conversion. It means trying and failing but always trying. Trying to do better, to be better, to love better, to forgive better. I am by no means perfect but I shudder to think how much worse I'd be without the influence of my faith!

And it's not a struggle undertaken alone. One is joined by a community of believers, living and deceased, and nourished on the journey by the Eucharist in which is manifested that great promise of Christ in Matthew's Gospel, 'I am with you always until the end of time.'

Knowing this helps one to move from the atheist Richard Dawkin's slogan of 'There's probably no God' to the response of the Chief Rabbi of the United Kingdom, Jonathan Sacks, that 'Improbably, there is a God'.

So, in short, Catholicism means everything.

Catholic?

Mark Patrick Hederman OSB

For nature then
To me was all in all – I cannot paint
What then I was. The sounding cataract
Haunted me like a passion; the tall rock,
The mountain, and the deep and gloomy wood,
Their colours and their forms, were then to me
An appetite; a feeling and a love,

But oft, in lonely rooms, and 'mid the din
Of towns and cities, I have owed to them
In hours of weariness, sensations sweet,
Felt in the blood, and felt along the heart

While with an eye made quiet by the power
Of harmony, and the deep power of joy,
We see into the life of things.

Wordsworth: *Lines Composed a Few Miles above Tintern Abbey*

Where I came from in Co. Limerick many of our friends were Protestants. This meant, in the 1950s, that we couldn't go to their funerals. The parish priest of Ballingarry, who lived until he was 106, told us, at the party for his hundredth birthday, that he only had two enemies during his long life: the English and the Protestants. Children in the parish were advised not to make friends with Protestants because it was basically a waste of time. Protestants would be going to hell and Catholics would never see them again for all eternity.

On the other hand, in the church where we went on Sundays in Granagh, the curate who preached was Father Sadlier who gave the best sermons I ever heard. I loved the prayers of the Mass, especially the one at the offertory, *Deus qui humane substantiae dignitatem et mirabiliter condidisti et mirabilius reformasti* (Oh, God who in creating human nature didst wonderfully dignify it and has still more wonderfully restored it). I had a direct relationship with God at a very early age and that relationship was expressed in the fields or on the mountaintop as much as in the church. Being Catholic was secondary, it happened to be the church into which I was born. The more primary and almost natural thing was immediate connection with God – meaning without intermediary – there was me and God and nothing of any great relevance in between.

I did not go to school until I was nine years of age; my American mother believed that children should not go to school until they themselves asked to do so. So the first nine years of my life were spent roaming the hillsides of West Limerick with my sister, Louise, mostly on ponies. In sight of the Galtee Mountains, between the Rivers Deel and Maigue, a ridge of old red sandstone rises abruptly from the limestone land of the surrounding area. This is *Cnoc Fírinne* (Hill of Truth), almost one thousand feet high. It was a short distance from our farm. Most of my childhood was spent around its vicinity. It had a cairn on top which is a large heap of stones added to by those who climb the hill. This cairn was called *an buachaill bréagach* (the deceitful boy). Near this cairn was an opening known as *Poll na Bruíne* which was an entrance to the underworld, the palace beneath the hill (*Brú na Bruíne*) where Donn Fíreannach presided. This word *Brú* occurs also in the names of towns in the locality, Bruree and Bruff for instance, and refers to such underground hostels as are found at the great megalithic site in the Boyne valley known as *Brú na Bóinne*. Many people around Ballingarry believed that there were underground tunnels from Cnoc Fírinne to the mouth of the Shannon, and up towards Tory Hill and beyond.

West Limerick is a place of high ringfort density south of the Shannon estuary. There was a ring fort on a forty-acre field at the edge of our own farm and a second one at Ballingarry Down on the approach to Knockfierna. I spent much time in both these places. Although it has been suggested that such forts were occupied from the Bronze Age (1800 BCE) more recent and more accurate dendrochronology and radiocarbon dating point to a period between 600 and 900 CE for the construction of most ringforts around Ireland. Whatever about their chronology or their construction, these were openings to another world. I later discovered that all cultures, and most children, around the world, believe in the existence of such a second dimension. In Africa the anthills of the Savannah were another variety of such openings. Knockfierna itself was the palace of Donn Fíreannach, God of the dead and of the fertility of the land, who was generally seen in our area on horseback.

A cross-country hurling match between the Slua Sí of Cnoc Fírinne led by Donn and the Slua Sí of Lough Gur and Cnoc Áine (Knockainey) led by the goddess Áine took place every autumn. The ball would be thrown in half-way between the two places, about fifteen miles between Knockfierna and Knockainey. If Donn succeeded in driving the ball back to Knockfierna the crops in this part of the country would thrive, but if Áine got the upper hand the people of Ballingarry could look out for themselves.

There is an account of Cearúil Ó Dálaigh (composer of *Eibhlín a Rúin*) travelling to Kilmallock to get Eibhlín to elope with him. He noticed a white horse going up the hill of Cnoc Fírinne. He followed it to the Poll Dubh where he found a horse grazing but no sign of its rider. He threw a stone down Poll na Bruíne. It was thrown back hitting him in the face and breaking his nose.

An old man who worked for my father told me that, coming back from church in Granagh, he heard 'fairy' music. As he looked through the low open window of his room out on Knockfierna, he knew that he would be there soon on the whale-backed Black Hill beside.

When eventually I went to school I was surprised to meet so many children because that is what they were. Being at school teaches us to be like children and to act that age. If you have lived all your life with adults you are not aware of the idiom. But you learn very quickly. I reverted to childhood within weeks. But the teachers here had no interest whatsoever in Donn Fíreannach or his buachaill bréagach. In fact they regarded all that as nonsense at the best of times and as heresy at the worst of times. And they had their ways of dealing with heretics. Every teacher in the school was armed with a different kind of sceptre or crozier for beating out heresy and converting the pagans. Pagans and heathens, I later learned, were all those who lived in the countryside (*paganus*) and dwelt on the heaths. As so many before me, I went into hiding like Heathcliff and became, as Jacob and Ulysses, a deceitful boy. At school there was only one world. It was measured by geometry (which means, in Greek, 'measuring the world') and counted in numbers which contained no magic. We sat in serried rows of passive clones for nine hours every day, supervised for the most part by one other person who brainwashed us continuously and beat us if we objected. Nine hours were spent asleep in dormitories and the remaining time was divided into organised games, meals or prayer.

The object was to help us 'get ahead' in the workaday world. We learned to read and write and then began the scientific con-quest of the space-time continuum in which we lived. Of course there was only one kind of space and only one kind of time. Both were absolute and invariant. There was no question of space being beyond us or time being inside us, no understanding of my space or your space, no appreciation of music as time being 'felt' or made audible, no such thing as time-for-us. This was an inventory of intelligible locations and dates, a map of the world for anthropologists anonymous. If you were living in any other kind of space and time, you were a dreamer, an idler, a good-for-nothing. The space we all lived in was an ordered totality of concrete extensions, the time we lived in was an ordered totality of concrete durations. Space, time and motion had been calculated for us; all we had to do was learn off the formulae. There was no time or space for 'my' world or 'your' world, for an overworld or an underworld, we were dealing with the 'real' world. We measured this in metres, kilograms, and seconds (MKS). The distance from Knockfierna to the ringfort was to be calculated in units which were one ten-millionth part of the meridian which passes from the pole to the equator. It didn't matter what anyone felt like, or what was going on underneath the ground. All that was subjective and personal. What we were after was an objective assessment – a picture of the world from nobody's point of view. If you arrive in London you don't want a sentimentally biased account of what someone else thinks you should see, you want a map which will show you where one wants to go and how to get there.

By the time I left school, of course, this attempt to reduce the world to signs and symbols which were unambiguous, incontrovertible and universally accepted, had already been changed. Just after my sixteenth birthday the standardised MKS of my rigid schooldays had been revised. The mouth of the Poll Dubh on Cnoc Fírinne was now to be measured in metres which were more accurately and scientifically accepted to be 1,650,753.73 wavelengths of the orange-red light of krypton 86.

The school I went to held a retreat every year for the boys who were boarders. We were asked to remain silent for three days and if we did so we would be given a free day at the end by the headmaster. Behind the main building there was a cultivated garden with a view of the Sugarloaf Mountain in Wicklow. This was supposed to be one of the most beautiful views in the country. It was too much of a picture post-card for me. It had nothing of the magic of Knockfierna. We could use the garden during the retreat to say the Rosary as we walked up and down. The way we said the Rosary was unusual. We divided ourselves into two teams. One team would begin saying the Rosary and the other would attack them and bring them to the ground shoving their faces into the earth until the Rosary was silenced. When eventually all sound of the Rosary had been eliminated it was the turn of the second team to stand up and begin the recital until they, in their turn, had been reduced to silence. In this way we fulfilled our obligations to pray without forfeiting our free day at the end by breaking the silence.

The retreat master, Father Gabriel Harty OP, was known as the Rosary Priest. After he had given his first talk I went to him and told him that he wasn't getting through to these boys at all. If he would let me give the next talk I would be able to tell them all about God in a way they might understand. He was very kind and told me that his next talk was going to involve showing a series of slides and that I could help him man the slide projector.

Knowledge of God was communicated through a *Catechism of Catholic Doctrine*, approved by the Archbishops and Bishops of Ireland, with an imprimatur from John Charles McQuaid, dated 2 February 1951. This catechism was learnt off by heart. The book was printed and bound in the Republic of Ireland. It began with The Sign of the Cross (An Indulgence of 100 days; with holy water, 300 days) and continued with 443 questions starting with 'Who made the world?' and 'Who is God?' and ending with 'What are exorcisms?' and 'What are the principal objects blessed by the Church for the use of the faithful?' ('water, palms, ashes, crucifixes, medals, rosaries and scapulars'). A local priest with a bamboo cane beat the answers into those who were slow or uninterested. I knew all the questions with their answers by rote and still do. They had very little, if anything, to do with my conversations on Knockfierna.

The second school I went to was Glenstal Abbey about fifty kilometres away from my home. I went at the age of twelve and remained there for the next fifty years apart from a series of absences which lasted in total not more than a decade. The reason why you go somewhere is rarely the reason why you stay. I am aware that one of the purposes of having a school in the monastery was to ensure the survival of the species. Boys were approached by monks whom they admired and told that lengthy consultations with the heavenly hierarchy had revealed that you were being considered as a suitable candidate for entry to the novitiate. Not all the boys were regarded as worthy of such canvassing but I was told by at least three different monks that my name was being mentioned in high places. Half of me was flattered that I should be discussed in the heavenly courts; the other half was horrified. I had always been interested in, and deeply aware of, God, but most of my conversations had been conducted on Knockfierna. I began to understand that it was impossible to be a mystic on a mountainside. I had to find a place.

Glenstal is a place. The name identifies the ghost of a male horse seen galloping through the archway of the castle. The Glen of the Stallion has been a hybrid place from its beginnings. Geographically and historically anomalous, it is situated in the countryside of south-east Limerick. Its landscape is dominated by a nineteenth century Norman castle pretending to be built in the twelfth century. Sir Charles Barrington selected the site so that each room on the south side of the castle would have a view of the Galtee Mountains. He constructed five artificial lakes around the castle to add the element of water to this landscape. The stone tower overlooking a panoramic vista, from the river Shannon on the east to the Galtee Mountains in the south, bears the name of the architect, Billy Barden, and the date of completion. 1138 is carved on the inner side of the tower beneath the parapet. Around the second number '1' a silhouetted figure of 8 is superimposed to soften the lie and circumlocute the truth. The mock castle appeared in the early nineteenth century. It was apparently built on the model of Windsor Castle outside London. Stone statues of Eleanor of Aquitaine and Henry II of France guard the front door to remind those who enter that they are now on planter land: this is Protestant territory inside a predominantly Catholic country and 'there is some corner of a foreign field/ that is forever England.' The grounds were designed as an earthly paradise. These gardens have since grown into a jungle and the ornamental rhododendrons designed as shrubs have escalated into colourful forests. The place has reverted to 'Irishry' by default.

Tragic circumstances of history caused the estate to change hands. The Barrington daughter, Winnie, was shot by mistake by the IRA who had ambushed her lover, a major in the British

Army stationed in Tipperary at that time. The family moved back to England and their beautiful castle and estate became a Benedictine monastery in 1927.

The Benedictines were founded in the sixth century after the fall of the Roman Empire. They have survived in most countries of the world in very beautiful places where they farm or teach, work and pray. Their form of prayer is liturgical and they otherwise go silently about their business. They have remained in silent liturgical praise of God, using ancient ceremonial and Latin chant right through the divisions which have marked the Christian Church. They somehow reach beyond these divisions and welcome all genuine seekers of God. In this sense they are Catholic, which means 'universal.'

Personally, I do not subscribe to a Catholicism which fails to live up to this name. And this means recognising that Judeo-christianity is one religion stemming from the revelation of the one God; that the break between Judaism and Christianity is similar to that between Protestantism and Catholicism; that Jews and Christians belong to the Catholicism which stems from the God of Abraham (also recognised by Moslems) and Isaac and Jacob, and which (in our view) reaches its culmination and fulfilment of revelation in Jesus Christ (the Messiah that Judaism has announced through its prophets), who is God Incarnate. The Church (the One, Holy, Catholic, and Apostolic) must, as an organisation, embody the Holy Spirit of Christ. Until it does so, it remains human, fallible and faulty, not yet having reached its full potential. I believe in God and I believe that the Holy Spirit is gradually improving the mechanisms which might change the Church from being the fragmented, self-opinionated, thick-headed, sexist, male-dominated organisation that cultural forces in our patriarchal world have allowed it to be, so that it may become eventually the transparent image of the God it was meant to be serving. I shall work as hard as I can to remove such dross and clean these windows, so that all manner of thing may be well, and that all may be one.

Coming to Terms with a Catholic Birthright

Mary O'Rourke

The first thing to say about my thoughts of being a Catholic is that I had no choice in the matter. I do not say this out of any sense of rebellion or antagonism. It's just a plain fact. I was born to a Catholic mother and father and therefore I was baptised, made my Holy Communion went to a nuns' primary school, went to a nuns' secondary school, made my Confirmation got married in a church. Similarly, my children were baptised in a church and like me they had no choice in the matter and so the cycle continues.

As I say, this is not said out of any sense of hostility or latent subversion. When I started thinking about what I would write, I said 'What does being a Catholic mean to me?' and I have to say, apart from the rituals of all of life's events as I have enumerated them in the above paragraph, it does not mean very much. I know that sounds bleak but it is the truth.

Looking back over my life now from the mighty age of seventy-two, can I remember my First Holy Communion day, and was I imbued with a sense of reverence? No, I can remember well my Communion Day and I was imbued with a sense of rage. My hair had been cut short to my scalp about a month before because there had been an outbreak of some sort of an infectious head disease in school and all the mothers of the little girls got notes to cut their children's hair. Mine was shaven to the bone. My mother lost the school note and in a frantic sense of motherly duties, shaved me tightly. So instead of having winsome curls, I had a veil clapped tight on my head from which stuck out about three pieces of hair which had begun to grow again. Hence, my justifiable sense of rage.

Did I feel the Holy Ghost descend upon me when I was making my Confirmation? No, not a bit of it again because we had now reached an age of jealousy of other girls and so I spent the time looking at what the other girls were wearing and wishing that I had worn something else.

On my wedding day, yes, I had a sense of reverence and anticipation. Reverence because I felt I was entering into a lifelong commitment and I was so so happy to be doing it with a person whom I desired so much and with whom I wished to spend my life. Anticipation because we had held off having sexual relations (as one did in those days) until we were married and I thought I would never get to lay my hands on him and he on me.

It did not work out immediately the way we wanted it to but that is another tale surely and not quite fit for this story, but all is well that ends well in that regard.

Although the cycle repeated itself with our two sons and all of the church rituals, I never thought to ask them if they had been imbued with reverence or any of the other worthy sentiments, but somehow I think not.

What does being a Catholic really mean to me? The normal ritual of a normal Mass does not excite me. Sometimes if I was at a funeral Mass the poignancy of the particular situation would strike me very forcibly and it would bring back the death of my husband Enda to me. I like the smell of incense in a church, I like the singing because it uplifts me. Interestingly enough, I have gone to a church here in Athlone which is the church of choice for the Nigerian Asylum Seekers whom we have in Athlone and they have their own native church, the Church of the Redeemer. They play music very loudly and they sing very loudly and every so often they break in to 'Lord be Praised, Alleluia, Alleluia' and it is joyful, cheerful and all carried on with great abandon. Amidst that, I can feel an affinity as I do not think the church was meant to be dull and cheerless.

There are two personal gripes I have with the operation of the present Catholic Church. The first is the anti-contraception doctrine which in the modern world is just plain silly. The second is the cold shoulder given to people who wish to marry again and who have been divorced. Yes, the law of the land allows them marry in a Registry Office (or whatever place ordained by the Registrars), but in a church, it is completely forbidden. Why? I ask myself. Why?

The use of Latin in the church rituals gave a sense of mystery to the proceedings. I have tried reading spiritual books but cannot gain anything from them. I would love to be able to feel in communion with God, to feel that he/she is there always for me but I can not bring myself to believe it.

Do I pray? Sadly, only when I need something very badly. I will say the lovely prayer from childhood, the Memorare, and say it with heartfelt passion or I will say the childish prayer 'Angel of God, my guardian dear, to whom God's love commits me here, ever this day be at my side, to light, to guard, to rule, and to guide. Amen' and I get comfort from that type of prayer. Sometimes I fear for the future and sometimes I dwell on what happens when we die, but I try not to think about it.

What is the afterlife to be when you are young and childish? You thought you would meet everyone you ever knew when you would die and go to heaven. I often had childish visions of flapping around in wings and bumping into people I knew from long ago. But I have no more time for those foolish notions. I prefer not to dwell on them but to look at the shining lovely faces of my five grandchildren and exult in their youth, their vigour, their charm, their innocence and their unquestioning love.

I never envisaged the joy I would get from my children's children. I relish every minute in their company. Every childish comment to my mind is potentially awesome in its wisdom. And so it goes on, a surge of constant love.

So how does a Catholic who does not feel Catholic live her life or what lode-star guides me on my way?

The sterility of the Catholic Church at present turns me off, or at least does not turn me on. Where can I look for comfort and solace? I do not want to sound pretentious but the Beatitudes as evidenced in both the Gospel of Matthew and the Gospel of

Luke have always seemed to me to be very good rules by which to abide. As we know Matthew's Gospel has nine beatitudes whereas Luke's has four, but taken in tandem they provide very potent headlines for a person in the modern world.

How happy are the poor in spirit:
theirs is the kingdom of heaven.
Happy the gentle:
they shall have the earth for their heritage.
Happy are those who mourn:
they shall be comforted.
Happy those who hunger and thirst for what is right:
they shall be satisfied.
Happy the merciful:
they shall have mercy shown them.
Happy the pure in heart:
they shall see God.
Happy the peacemakers:
they shall be called children of God.
Happy those who are persecuted in the cause of right:
theirs is the kingdom of heaven.
Happy are you when people abuse you and persecute you
and speak all kinds of calumny against you on my account.
Rejoice and be glad, for your reward will be great in heaven.

Read any one of the above and it is certainly modern, heady, and compelling in what it is saying to us through the gospels.

I know it would be impossible for anyone to measure up to those Beatitudes, but they are like a beautiful sermon which when read or heard lingers in your mind. All we can hope to do in life is to live according to our own inner spirit and discipline.

When I read these Beatitudes, doubt goes from my mind. I feel that the afterlife will consist of being forever in the presence (though not bodily) of something that is beautiful and right and proper; in other words, God. Call this escapism if you want to. But is it any more escapism than the feeling that there is somewhere over the rainbow where skies are always blue?

CHAPTER TWENTY-ONE

I Loved my Church Once

Colm O'Gorman

I'm not Catholic anymore. I never formally quit the Church or anything; I just came to realise that I was no longer part of it. I didn't write to a bishop or the Pope, didn't go through a defined process through which I renounced my allegiance to the 'one holy, catholic and apostolic Church'. I reckon that if my entry by proxy as an infant was valid, then my mature and considered decision to leave was certainly at least as valid and not at all subject to the demands for signed declarations from men who, for me, no longer held any moral authority.

I've been asked a lot over the years if I still consider myself to be Catholic, and my answer was always the same. No, I no longer do. And yet there is something so very real about writing it in the context of this essay that feels emotional to me, a realisation perhaps of the enormity of that decision and the events which led to it. I have felt clear in my decision; in fact it has been clear to me for some time that I could not possibly belong to this Church which has at an institutional level so betrayed me and the values it has professed, but nevertheless in considering this essay I have had cause to reflect back upon what the Church has meant to me across my life, and I am left feeling hurt and saddened in many ways.

There was a Sacred Heart picture in our kitchen when I was a boy. It had a flickering red light beneath the image of Christ who exposed his heart surrounded by thorns, a symbol of divine love for humanity. I didn't know what it represented as a boy, but I could see that it was about love, about a demonstration of love on a powerful level that I couldn't understand fully but felt captured by completely. That image was a gentle but extraordinarily powerful presence in our home, as it was in most Catholic homes at the time. I loved it, though I didn't really understand it.

Church was everywhere in my life then. At home as we knelt as a family to say the Rosary, at school as I learnt my catechism and at Mass on Sundays where I went with the rest of my family dressed in our Sunday best. Our church was a very ordered place back then. The women sat on the left hand side of the church, many with their heads covered by scarves, and the men on the right. Boys sat with their fathers and girls with their mothers. A few rows of men, maybe two or three deep, always stood at the back of the church. As the Mass came to an end they would duck out and head for the pub next door, for that other Sunday ritual, the after-Mass pint. They were an incongruous crowd, standing together at the back of the church, shuffling and mumbling their way through the Mass, waiting to be released. But they were there, week in, week out, just as their fathers before them. It was who they were. It was who we all were.

I loved the rituals of the Church. I loved the certainty of them. The way Father Redmond would intone the words of the Mass, the weight of those words, words which spanned two millennia and which celebrated a great sacrifice, the sacrifice of a son for the love of humanity. The reverence of it all, the way we knelt with heads bowed as Father Redmond held aloft the host and the altar boy rang the bell to mark the moment of transubstantiation, when the bread became flesh and the wine became blood, when we were all in the presence of Christ. I was in awe of that sacrifice, of the love it was testament to, a love of humanity so great that God would give the life of his only Son. This was a loving God, a God of hope and truth.

I sometimes struggled with the messages I was given by those who instructed me on that faith. I found it difficult to reconcile that idea of a loving God with the heavy judgement of Original Sin or the notion that only by allegiance to this Church could I find redemption. I loved the God that loved, that so believed in us that he was prepared to sacrifice his Son for us. I didn't understand this other God who was to be feared and who would cast me out if I proved not to be worthy of him. But that was how it was. I was taught that I was bad, that I was sinful and that my redemption from my sinful state was to be found by allegiance to those who spoke the words of God. If I did as I was told I could be saved from my base self; I could be made good again.

And that is what I believed. I believed that those who spoke the words of God were good and true and pure, even when they were not. I believed it because that is what I was required to believe. That was the truth of the world in which I lived and there was no room for other beliefs. That is what everyone believed, so who was I to disagree?

Imagine then how it was when a priest raped me. How was I to make sense of that? If he was undoubtedly good in the eyes of all, then how was I to understand what had happened? There was only one way. I was bad. It was me, not the priest. I was the sinful one, the one in need of redemption, redemption that was in his gift. And so it was. I judged myself as I had been judged and took on the guilt of the sin that wasn't mine. I carried it for years, turned it in on myself and it festered there, in a place where love did not exist, where God could surely not be found.

Years later I fought my way back to love. I confronted that past and forgave myself for crimes that I had not committed. I learnt to love myself and have compassion for the boy I was and the man I had become. I found out I wasn't so bad after all.

The tragedy is that I did not discover this through a communion with my Church. In fact, I discovered it despite the actions of that Church.

When I realised that I needed to speak about the things that had happened to me as a boy I had no idea of the complicity of the Church. I did not know that the man who so harmed me had been ordained despite the knowledge that he had abused children. I did not know that my Church had stood on the sidelines as he raped and abused, that it had looked away, taking action only to protect itself and its money and leaving me and countless others at the mercy of monsters it had helped to create. I did not know, but those who led my Church did, and they stayed silent in the presence of my pain. They did not speak, they did not own up to their crimes or try to comfort me. There was no love; no sacred heart that bled for those whose innocence and faith had been so offended.

When I turned to the Church that purported to be the Church of the loving Christ, I was not met with love and truth, but with lies and obfuscation.

The denial and deceit of the hierarchy of the institutional Catholic Church was a final and terrible revelation of the corruption of its values by those who lead it. How could I trust the word of men who lied about their knowledge of such crimes and who facilitated the rape and abuse of children? For years bishops, cardinals and both the current and former popes had suggested that the problem didn't exist, or that it was wildly overstated by an anti-Catholic media, or that it was an issue of homosexuals in the clergy, or most often, that they had no understanding of the reality of child sexual abuse and the recidivist nature of offenders.

But these were lies.

In early December 2002, Cardinal Joseph Ratzinger, now Pope Benedict XVI, made a staggering statement suggesting that media coverage of clerical sexual abuse was a conspiracy to bring down the Roman Catholic Church.

The current Pope was then Prefect of the Congregation for the Doctrine of the Faith. In that powerful and influential role he was often referred to as God's Rottweiler or the Vatican Enforcer. His position as head of the department once known as the Holy Office of the Inquisition placed him in charge of managing and responding to cases of priests who abused children.

More than any other senior Church figure apart from the Pope, he had both the authority and knowledge to appreciate fully the scale of the problem. Speaking to journalists at a Catholic Congress in Rome, he said, 'I am personally convinced that the constant presence in the press of the sins of Catholic priests, especially in the United States, is a planned campaign, as the percentage of these offences among priests is not higher than in other categories, and perhaps it is even lower. In the United States, there is constant news on this topic, but less than 1% of priests are guilty of acts of this type.' He continued: 'The constant presence of these news items does not correspond to the objectivity of the information nor to the statistical objectivity of the facts. Therefore, one comes to the conclusion that it is intentional, manipulated, that there is a desire to discredit the Church. It is a logical and well-founded conclusion.'

So in his view the truth was not that he and his colleagues who presided over the Church had covered up the rape and abuse of children, allowing paedophile priests to wreak havoc with virtual impunity. In fact, the real issue as he saw it was as 'a planned campaign ... intentional ... manipulated', based not upon outrage at the sins and crimes of the Catholic Church, but upon a 'desire to discredit the Church'.

Cardinal Ratzinger's assertions were entirely discredited a few years later by research in the United States. In June 2002, US Bishops commissioned independent research into the scale of the problem. The research was carried out by the John Jay College of Criminal Justice and found that clerical sexual abuse was 'widespread' across the US Catholic Church, affecting some ninety-five percent of dioceses and involving between two and a half and seven percent of all diocesan priests. Overall, the research discovered that four percent of all priests in active ministry in the US between 1952 and 2002 had been accused of sexually abusing a child.

The study also revealed that of the 10,667 people who made allegations of rape and abuse by priests, two thirds had been made prior to 2002. This means that in the US alone, the Catholic Church was aware of over 7,100 cases of children allegedly abused by its priests prior to the public emergence of the issue.

Early Church law also reveals that the Catholic Church has had an awareness of clerical sexual crime going back many centuries. The earliest reference to forbidden sexual behaviour in church literature dates from around the end of the first century. The *Didache*, which set out structures and rules for the newly emerging Church, condemns many sexual practices and includes a specific ban against 'corrupting youth'.

Many early church laws relate to sex with adult women and homosexuality, but there are also frequent references to the crime of sexually abusing boys. Sexual sins ranked as high as murder and idolatry in early Church law, the three gravest sexual sins being adultery, fornication and the sexual corruption of young boys. In fact, some of the earliest church law refers explicitly to that crime. The Council of Elvira, which took place in 309AD, set out early Church law in the area, detailing how clergy were to abstain from sexual offending under this new law. Canon seventy-one of the Council of Elvira condemns men who sexually abuse young boys and sets out the penalty for the crime.

In 1051, St Peter Damian, a monk who became a bishop and later a cardinal, wrote extensively about the sexual crimes and immorality of the clergy of his day. His strongest criticism was of the irresponsibility of Church superiors who refused to take action against offenders. He condemned homosexual activity by clergy, but clergy who abused young boys especially angered him. He attacked Church superiors who ordained offenders and who failed to expel those who abuse from the priesthood. He also made a direct appeal to the reigning Pope, Leo IX, to take action.

No doubt, then, what this eleventh century bishop would have had to say about his modern day brother bishops and cardinals who ordained abusers and appointed them to parish after parish, thus allowing them to rape and abuse with near impunity.

On 30 August 1568, another Pope explicitly acknowledged the issue of clergy abusing children. In his papal order *Horrendum*, Pope Pius V said that priests who offended were to be stripped of the priesthood, deprived of all income and privileges and handed over to the secular authorities.

There are scores of other references to the issue throughout Catholic Church history that expose as a lie the many statements made by the modern Catholic Church hierarchy claiming innocence and ignorance. They have known for centuries that priests could and did abuse children. They simply failed to do anything of any real significance to prevent it.

I loved my Church once, when I believed in it. But I do not anymore. It gives me no pleasure to say so, no satisfaction or closure. I remember the Sacred Heart picture in the kitchen of my childhood, the faith of my grandmother, the power of the sacraments, the constant presence of the faith as an anchor in all of our lives. I remember how we looked to Church to make real the momentous moments of our lives – birth, marriage and death. I remember the faith of my forefathers and I feel nothing but sadness.

CHAPTER TWENTY-TWO

'Reverting' to Catholicism

David Quinn

In some ways I am what is called a 'revert'. That is to say, I had
drifted away from Catholicism and later returned to it.

In Catholic terms my upbringing was conventional enough.
My mother was a Limerick woman and like most women of her
generation, was a full-time housewife. She was fairly pious, but
not extremely so. As a child I can remember her praying by the
side of her bed before climbing in. She would try to get myself
and my three sisters to say the Angelus and grace before meals.
She gave up the attempt fairly early on because we were so resistant. Thinking back, I don't even know why we were resistant.
Maybe we found praying boring.

We would go to Mass every week and it was entirely a routine affair for us. It was something you did because you did it.
We put no thought into the act one way or the other. But there
were no holy pictures on the walls of our home. We never said
the Rosary or were brought along to Mass on anything other
than Sundays and Holy Days. No attempt was made to instruct
us in the faith. I think it was assumed we were picking that up in
school.

My father, who was born and raised in Dublin, was a journalist, as was his father. He came along to Mass with the rest of us
each week but I never got the impression that religion meant a
great deal to him. He wasn't especially for it, nor was he especially against it. It was simply something that was there, like the
weather. It was good when it was good, and bad when it was
bad.

We had no priests or religious on either side of our family
except for a distant cousin or two whom we never saw. The only

priests and nuns we ever came across were in the local schools or parishes. I can't ever remember any coming into the house.

I began school in the local Holy Faith convent in Clontarf. A lot of convent schools back then educated boys up to First Class. I would have started school in 1967 and back then all the nuns wore their habits. Our teacher was a lay-woman. I vaguely remember being taught the old-style penny catechism with its questions and answers in the very early days but it disappeared along with the Latin Mass which I can't remember at all.

Then it was on to St Paul's College, Raheny, where I spent eleven years. St Paul's is run by the Vincentians who, in my experience, were a very benign lot. Corporal punishment was only used sparingly and as a result I never dreaded going to school.

We had a teacher in Fifth and Sixth Class who was very old-school with a fondness for taking a ruler, turning it on its side and striking you over the tips of the fingers if you stepped out of line. He was determined to teach us Irish and religion above all. I hated Irish because I've never had a flair for languages – worse luck. But some of the religion he taught us stuck.

In secondary school religion was a hit and miss affair. There seemed to be no religion text-books that I can recall. I think religious education was in a sort of limbo back then. The old style of teaching religion had gone but nothing new had replaced it so what happened in class was very much up to the teacher.

I left school in 1981 and studied business at Dublin City University (the National Institute for Higher Education as it was at the time). Except for going to Mass on Sunday, religion played absolutely no part in my life during my time at DCU. It wasn't that I was against religion. It was just that it meant very little to me or to most of my friends. We rarely talked about it even though we were interested in current affairs.

I was still in DCU at the time of the first abortion referendum in 1983 and followed it only at a distance. There were a few debates about it at the lunch-table but they were half-hearted affairs. The debates about Ronald Reagan's foreign policy were much more full-throated. I didn't vote at all in the referendum of that year. I didn't like either side and wasn't much interested in those sorts of social issues. What a contrast with today!

Of course, in the 1980s the overwhelming issue for university students was the state of the economy, which was appalling, and where we would go when we graduated. Lots of us went overseas. I went to Australia, along with a fellow graduate. This was my first time away from home for any serious length of time and apart from a Sunday here or there week, I stopped going to Mass. It was from sheer laziness. I credit myself for not pretending it was out of principle. At the same time, it was Australia that aroused my interest in religion for the first time in any genuine sense which is a strange thing to say because Australia was, and still is, so much more secular than Ireland.

But I think it did it for three main reasons. The least important reason is that for the first time I was living in a country in which the Catholic Church did not play a dominant role and yet Australia had some of the same problems as Ireland in addition to a set of other problems I had never come across before, such as a high rate of divorce. Back home, I never had much patience for the argument that the Catholic Church was responsible for all our problems and Australia convinced me further of this and freed me from the 'blame the Catholic Church for everything' attitude that seemed quite prevalent back home. It also told me that if the conventional wisdom (among many of my peers at any rate), could be wrong about this, it could be wrong about a whole lot else besides.

A second reason is that while working in Sydney I met a fellow by the name of Thomas Shaw whom I've lost contact with unfortunately. Thomas, who was my own age, was one of the best read and most reflective people I had ever come across and he had a special talent for forcing a person to consider what they believed and why. He forced a person to consider their presuppositions, to make them visible so that the person could decide whether these presuppositions were credible. He did this in a very gentle way. Thomas himself had a more or less New Age view of the world, but it was unobtrusive and not in the least 'flaky'. But he was sympathetic to all religious expressions, unlike some adherents of the New Age who are very hostile towards Christianity. Thomas showed me that I hadn't worked out whether my basic view of the world was secular or religious. I was somewhere in between. I had some thinking to do.

The final piece of the jigsaw fell into place when I met my wife-to-be, who was a Protestant. In the first flush of love I was happy to trot along to her church and this brought me into proper contact for the first time with another Christian tradition and it impressed me enormously.

By now I had decided that my basic worldview was religious. I believed in God. I was a Christian. But what kind of Christian? A bad one, undoubtedly, but what were my beliefs? Rachael's Protestant Church made me explore the basic questions over which Protestants and Catholics have argued, and sometimes fought, for the last five hundred years and after much reading I came down on the Catholic side.

By now I was around twenty-five and for the first time I had something approaching a proper appreciation of Catholicism and I remember being mildly resentful that no-one had given me a proper appreciation of it before. I read Catholic and non-Catholic writers. I loved C. S. Lewis – a member of the Church of England – for his clarity. And brevity. He tackled lots of the tough questions such as why is there suffering, do miracles happen, is the resurrection credible, what about the incarnation? G. K. Chesterton, I discovered, had a genius for taking the secular criticisms of Christianity and inverting them. For example, today Christianity is attacked for being too anti-sex, but at times in the past it was attacked for being too pro-sex. The Church doesn't believe sex or the body is evil, but the Cathars did, and they attacked the Church for believing otherwise.

Today it is assaulted precisely for hating sex and hating the body, but in fact the Church simply takes the view that sex has a context – marriage – which gives it is fullest meaning and reveals its true purpose which is both unitative and procreative. It leads to love and it leads to life. What could be more positive? In fact, this leads me on to my current main area of interest; marriage and the family, a core area of Church teaching that is one reason why I remain a Catholic.

When you come to think of it, half the problems we make for ourselves are the result of abandoning the Christian view of sex. Modern sexual ethics is all about maximising personal freedom. As this thinking would have it, two or more consenting adults should be allowed to do whatever they want, sexually speaking. But modern sexual mores often come at the expense of an ethic of commitment. By putting sex first and commitment second, women often find themselves literally holding the baby, alone. The child has no father, or at least not one willing to commit to it. The woman has no husband, or partner. Finding herself alone, if she is desperate enough the baby might be aborted.

When sex comes first and love and commitment, not to mention marriage, come second, the chances of being hurt emotionally increase exponentially. One person, often the woman, invests emotionally in the relationship, such as it is. But the other person, often the man, isn't invested in it at all and when he pulls the plug his partner is left feeling badly hurt and let down. Christian sexual morality isn't actually a series of dos and don'ts. It is actually aimed at maximising the welfare of the family and all its members. If a couple commit to one another first, before having sex, the chances of one or other being emotionally hurt diminishes enormously and any child they have will have two committed parents from the first day of their lives.

Of course, marriages don't always work out but a society with a healthy marriage culture is a healthy society. Such a society will have far fewer hurt people, especially children. Our society puts adults and their freedom first, and child and their welfare second. When the Church is accused of being obsessed with sex the accusation misses the mark. It isn't obsessed with sex, it is concerned about the family, as it ought to be because for most people nothing is more important than the family they were raised in and the family they form.

Of course, these days the Church is attacked for being intolerant towards families that are not based on marriage. But the Church has to give priority to the family based on marriage because children tend to fare best when raised by a loving mother and father who are married. The Church has to help all families that need help, but the best way to help the family per se, is to encourage marriage.

I've devoted a few hundred words to the question of the family because this question now takes up a large part of my time, and because it is so topical and because it is so vital. If the Church had no real wisdom to offer on this score then of what real use could it be? If it is wrong about the family, then its whole anthropology, its whole view of human nature, is wrong and if it is wrong about so crucial a question, then it might be wrong about much else besides and it must be man-made, not God-given.

Pope John Paul II insisted that we had to get our anthropology right, or we get almost everything else wrong. This was his chief criticism of communism. Communism saw man as a purely material creature and also one that was infinitely malleable by society. Having got that so badly wrong, how could it not collapse? With regard to communism, the Church's anthropology was spot-on and it is the same with regard to the family. This will be proven over time as people come again to realise that sex has a physical, an emotional and a reproductive dimension that ought ideally to be tied together in the totality of a sexual relationship in order to maximise the welfare of the adults involved, and especially of any children they might have together.

But naturally, in the end, Christianity is not simply an ethical system. Ultimately it is about a relationship with a person, namely Jesus Christ, and a Christian, an orthodox one at any rate, will answer certain questions about Jesus in a particular way. For example, that Jesus is True God and True Man, and is the Saviour of the world. We believe that Jesus is worth imitating as best we can and with the help of grace. As Catholics we believe we belong to a community that traces itself directly back to Jesus and his first followers and that this community has developed certain beliefs about Jesus and what it means to follow him.

No one can deny that the Catholic Church, or rather some of its adherents, have been guilty of terrible acts down the centuries, not least the child abuse scandals. This makes it hard to be a Catholic. In fact, it is extremely difficult to be a Catholic right now, in early twenty-first century Ireland. A lot of the time you have to hang your head in shame. But many of us are all simply hanging on as well. We do so because we believe in God, we believe in Jesus Christ and we believe the seed that eventually became the Catholic Church as we now know it was planted by Christ. We also hang on in there because there are so many good people in the Church but who are mostly unsung and uncelebrated. They are often our mothers and our fathers, our brothers and our sisters, our friends and neighbours and relatives. We see how their lives have been strengthened, enriched and improved by the faith in God and in Jesus that the Catholic Church helps to build and to develop. We can often take this for granted. We shouldn't. We should appreciate it and be grateful for it.

Editors and Contributors

EDITORS

John Littleton, a priest of the Diocese of Cashel and Emily, is Head of Distance Education at The Priory Institute, Tallaght, Dublin. With Eamon Maher, he co-edited *Irish and Catholic? Towards Understanding an Identity* (The Columba Press, 2006) and *Contemporary Catholicism in Ireland: A Critical Appraisal* (The Columba Press, 2008). He is a weekly columnist with *The Catholic Times*.

Eamon Maher is Director of the National Centre for Franco-Irish Studies in IT Tallaght. He is editor of *The Reimagining Ireland* book series with Peter Lang (Oxford) and his most recent edited book, *Cultural Perspectives on Globalisation and Ireland*, is published in this series. He is currently writing a second monograph on John McGahern entitled, *'The Church and its Spire': John McGahern and the Catholic Question*, for The Columba Press.

CONTRIBUTORS

Conor Brady worked as a journalist, broadcaster and editor for more than forty years. From 1986 to 2002 he was editor of *The Irish Times*. In 2006 he was appointed by the President of Ireland, on the nomination of the Houses of the Oireachtas, to be one of three Commissioners of the newly-established Garda Síochána Ombudsman Commission.

Finola Bruton is married to the former Taoiseach John Bruton and is the mother of four children.

Patricia Casey is Professor of Psychiatry at UCD and Consultant Psychiatrist in the Mater Misericordiae University Hospital. She is the author of five academic books and contributor to over thirty others.

Thomas Finegan is working as a parliamentary assistant in Seanad Éireann. He studied theology and philosophy, and is now researching for a PhD in the law school, Trinity College, Dublin.

Mark Patrick Hederman is Abbot of Glenstal Abbey and the author of several books.

Seán Kelly is a former President of the GAA and has recently been elected to the European Parliament for the Munster constituency.

Mary T. Malone has been retired in Ireland for a decade after thirty years of teaching Church history and feminist theology in the Toronto area of Canada.

Enda McDonagh is a priest of the Archdiocese of Tuam, and former Professor of Moral Theology at Maynooth. He rececently edited, with Vincent Mac Namara, *An Irish Reader in Moral Theology* (The Columba Press, 2009).

Patsy McGarry is Religious Affairs Correspondent with *The Irish Times*. He has written several books, the most recent of which is *First Citizen: Mary McAleese and the Irish Presidency* (O'Brien Press, 2008).

Peter McVerry is a Jesuit priest who has been working with homeless young people and drug users for the past thirty years. He writes regularly on social issues in Irish society and on the relationship between our Christian faith and justice.

Andrew O'Connell is employed by the Presentation Brothers to communicate faith and promote an understanding of vocation among young adults and in parishes.

Mary O'Donnell recently published her sixth collection of poetry, *The Ark Builder* (Ark Publishing, 2009). Her most recent fiction is *Storm over Belfast* (New Island, 2008). She was elected to membership of Aosdána in 2001. www.maryodonnell.com

Colm O'Gorman is the founder and former Director of One in Four. He is currently the Executive Director of Amnesty International Ireland and is also the author of a memoir, *Beyond Belief*. He writes here in a personal capacity.

Nuala O'Loan is a former Police Ombudsman for Northern Ireland.

Mary O'Rourke TD was appointed Minister in different Fianna Fáil-led governments and was leader of the Seanad from 2002 to 2007.

Garry O'Sullivan is Managing Editor of *The Irish Catholic*, has worked as a journalist in New York and Rome and has written extensively for the *Irish Independent*.

David Quinn is Director of the Iona Institute and a columnist with the *Irish Independent*. He also worked as editor of *The Irish Catholic* for several years and still writes for that newspaper.

William Reville is Associate Professor of Biochemistry and Public Awareness of Science Officer at University College Cork. He is also a columnist with *The Irish Times*.

Brendan Ryan spent two years in the novitiate of the Divine Word Missionaries. He has worked as a Lecturer in Chemical Engineering in Cork Institute of Technology from 1973 to date. He was a Senator for twenty-two years between 1981 and 2007.

Aidan Troy is a Passionist priest who is a native of Bray, Co. Wicklow. He has been parish priest of St Joseph's Church, Paris, since October 2008. From 2001 to 2008 he was at Holy Cross, Belfast.

D. Vincent Twomey SVD, Professor Emeritus of Moral Theology, is the author of *The End of Irish Catholicism?* (Veritas, 2003) and *Pope Benedict XVI: The Conscience of Our Age* (Ignatius Press, 2007).

John Waters is an author and columnist with *The Irish Times*. His latest book, *Beyond Consolation*, an exploration of the language of hope in contemporary Irish culture, will be published by Continuum in February 2010.